IN PRAISE
—— OF ——
DECADENCE

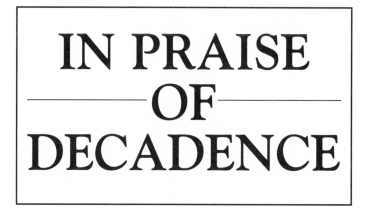

IN PRAISE

—OF—

DECADENCE

Jeff Riggenbach

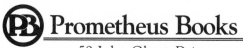 Prometheus Books
59 John Glenn Drive
Amherst, New York 14228-2197

Published 1998 by Prometheus Books

02 01 00 99 98   5 4 3 2 1

Library of Congress Cataloging-in-Publication Data

Riggenbach, Jeff.
    In praise of decadence / Jeff Riggenbach.
        p.   cm.
    Includes bibliographical references and index.
    ISBN 1–57392–246–3 (cloth : alk. paper)
    1. Social values—United States—History—20th century. 2. Political culture—United States—History—20th century. 3. Nineteen sixties. 4. Liberty—United States. 5. Individualism—United States. I. Title.
HN58.R53   1998
306′.0973′0904—dc21   98–37930
                                                                                              CIP

Printed by Edwards Brothers in the United States of America on acid-free paper

This book is for

Roy A. Childs Jr. (1949–1992)

and

Suzanne Hoy Riggenbach,

who made it possible.

Contents

Acknowledgments

Preliminary versions of some of the chapters in this book appeared originally in the *Libertarian Review*: "In Praise of Decadence" (February 1979), "Calling the Kettles Black" (June 1979), "Degeneration Revisited" (January 1980), "The Politics of Aquarius" (March 1981); and *Reason*: "The Disowned Children of Ayn Rand" (December 1982), "Vroom to Grow" (January 1983), "Family Fever" (June–July 1984), "Talkin' 'Bout My G-Generation" (May 1988).

Part One

In Praise of Decadence

1

The Legacy of the Sixties

The year, the decade, the century, the millennium—all are nearly spent. And behold! They who almost never agree are suddenly in firm and fundamental agreement. Over the past fifteen years or so, very slowly but also quite surely, an unmistakable consensus has actually begun to emerge from the ranks of those notoriously captious and disagreeable critics and commentators, those legendarily quarrelsome and disputatious pundits and polemicists, who specialize in defining the Zeitgeist, the Spirit of the Age, the State of the Culture. Liberal and conservative alike, whatever and however intensely felt their many differences may be, they are of one and only one mind as to this one point: we are what and as we are today because of the ways in which we have reacted to the legacy of the fabled 1960s.

For most contemporary liberals, our age is best characterized as a kind of "sellout" by former liberals and others formerly on the Left who have reacted against the very values and ideals they themselves once held dear, betraying the communitarian and egalitarian vision that inspired them back in the '60s, during their student days, in favor of (to put it bluntly) selfishness: the "Human Potential Movement" of the infamous "Me Decade" of the 1970s, the brazenly acquisitive "yuppie" lifestyle of the 1980s, and the "socially irresponsible greed" of the 1990s.

For most contemporary conservatives, our age is best understood as a traditionalist backlash; a disgusted, terminally fed-up reaction against the left-liberal "permissiveness" that became fashionable during the '60s.

Central to both these conceptions is the belief that it was the rebellious young people of the time—the war resisters and the flower children, the draft-card burners, the pot smokers, and the campus radicals—who made that tumultuous and incredible decade what it was.

To me, some such belief as this seems virtually inescapable. But there are a few people—most commonly they are people who played no part themselves in the political demonstrations, "sit-ins," "be-ins," "love-ins," and assorted "countercultural" activities and events of twenty to twenty-five years ago, whether because they were too old, too young, too unsympathetic, too cynical, or merely too wrapped up in their own personal lives and problems to have time for public issues and public events of any kind—who argue otherwise.

"It was only a small minority of the American population," these people argue, "that participated in antiwar demonstrations during the 1960s. It was only a small minority of Americans that became 'hippies' or got involved with illegal drugs or stopped cutting their hair and shaving their beards or cultivated the habit of referring to police officers as 'pigs.' Most Americans—including most of those who were in their late teens and early twenties at the time—lived through the '60s in exactly the same way they had lived through the '50s: in accord with traditional values and traditional ways of living and doing things.

"Throughout the '60s and early '70s, however, the mass media devoted a great deal of airtime and a great many column inches to coverage of the unsavory activities of what was really only a handful of unwashed, ill-mannered young people. And this unbalanced media coverage succeeded in convincing many Americans that the unruly behavior of this handful of people was actually typical of the decade as a whole. In fact, it was *a*typical of that decade, just as it had always been atypical of every decade of American history up to that time, and just as it has been atypical of every decade of American history since then. Every generation of college students has included its share of radicals and rebels and nonconformists. The students of the '60s were no different in this respect from the students of the 1930s or the 1910s or even the 1860s. There were student antidraft demonstrations during the Civil War, and again during World War I. The only difference is that when the same thing happened again in the 1960s, it was blown up out of all proportion by the media."

There is *some* truth in this argument. The majority of adolescent and young adult Americans *did* go right on leading their lives in traditional ways during the 1960s. It *was* only a minority of the American populace which became involved in the political and cultural rebellions the mass media covered so extensively at the time. And radicals, rebels, and nonconformists *have* been part of every generation of college students known to history.

In point of fact, every generation in human history seems to have been convinced that "the younger generation" of its time was going to hell in a handbasket. Any reader who plows his or her way through a few hundred years worth of published comments on "the younger generation" will find it difficult to resist the conclusion that the human condition has been steadily growing worse and worse for centuries. There were many "solid citizens" in the America of the 1920s who felt about the goldfish-swallowing, telephone booth-stuffing, *American Mercury*-reading, speakeasy-patronizing, Prohibition-flouting college students of that time exactly as the "solid citizens" of the America of the 1960s felt about the student rebels of their era.

However, the difference between what happened in the 1960s and what happened during the 1920s—or during the First World War or the American Civil War—is *not* merely a difference in the way events were portrayed by the mass media. For there are two other differences that set the '60s completely apart from these earlier periods.

First, there is the utterly unprecedented size, relative to the size of the U.S. population as a whole, of the college-age generation of the '60s.

Second, there is the fact that the youth rebellion of the '60s was actually two entirely separate and distinct rebellions—one of them political, the other broadly cultural—both of which, from the very beginning, have been utterly and completely misconceived and misunderstood.

2

The Baby Boomers

The birthrate in the United States has been declining for more than two centuries, since around the time of the American Revolution—except for a single brief period about two decades in length, between 1946 and 1964, when, suddenly, unexpectedly, something extraordinary happened. All at once, shortly after the end of World War II, the birth rate, which had been going down for as long as anyone could remember, more than doubled. It held steady at its new level for nearly twenty years, then collapsed—falling back, all at once, to the old, more familiar level of a little less than two children per woman of childbearing age. And it has declined relentlessly, despite intermittent fluctuations, ever since.

Because the generation of persons born during this period (1946 to 1964)—the "baby boom generation," as it has come to be called—was both preceded and followed by much smaller generations, it has formed a sort of permanent, moving bulge in the U.S. population. As Landon Y. Jones put it in *Great Expectations: America and the Baby Boom Generation* (1980), demographers use the vaguely discomfiting metaphor of a "pig in a python" to describe the resulting motion of the baby-boom bulge through the decades as it ages. But peristalsis, as that digestive process is called, hardly does justice to the violence and disruption felt along the way—by both pig and python.[1]

The disruption has been gigantic indeed, and far-reaching in its effects. In Jones's words, "much of our history over the past thirty years amounts to our generally unsuccessful effort to accommodate and absorb its [the baby boom generation's] enormous number."

During the years when the baby boom Americans were babies, the baby food and baby furniture businesses—and, of course, the diaper industry—all boomed incredibly, only to sag just as incredibly when their customers became housebroken and went off to school. Then, during their years in school, the school-building and teacher-certifying industries boomed incredibly, only to sag just as incredibly when their customers began entering college. It wasn't long before primary and secondary schools all over the country were closing their doors for lack of business and unemployed teachers were becoming nearly as common as unemployed black teenagers.

And, of course, during the baby boomers' college years, what you might call the "political demonstration business" boomed incredibly. The mass media neither invented nor exaggerated this boom in the business of organizing and staging rallies and marches; circulating petitions and burning draft cards; occupying buildings and distributing leaflets, broadsides, and other publications in support of "The Movement." Because of the uncommon size of the baby boom generation, not only were there more young people of college age in the U.S. population after 1964 than there had ever been before—also, and more important, young people of college age constituted a much larger proportion of the total population after 1964 than people of that age had ever constituted before.

Clearly, then, even if political activism was no more common among adolescent baby boomers than among adolescents of any other generation, the fact that the baby boomers were so much more numerous would tend to make their political activism more noticeable, more conspicuous, than the political activism of smaller generations had ever been in the past. It wasn't just a figment of the mass media's fevered imagination: there really *were* more kids out there in the streets fighting political battles during the '60s than there ever had been before.

3

Left, Right, or Libertarian?

On the other hand, it is undeniable that the mass media's coverage of the student political activism of the '60s *was* distorted and misleading at the time that activism was going on. From the very beginning, to cite only one of the many available examples, the mass media consistently portrayed "The Movement" as an expression of the values and ideals of the "New Left," and consistently depicted certain leaders of the student Left of the 1960s as leaders of contemporary student political opinion in general. And in the years since, this notion that the student political rebellion of the '60s was a rebellion of the Left has gone on to become nothing less than a never-questioned commonplace of the Conventional Wisdom—one of those exasperating propositions which "everybody knows" to be true and which is therefore never exposed for the flagrant falsehood it really is, for there is little or no incentive to check the actual facts in a case where "everybody knows" already what the truth of the matter is.

In fact, the student political activists of the 1960s were *never,* except briefly and incidentally, fighting for the values and ideals of the Left. The problem was, the values and ideals they *were* fighting for no longer had any generally agreed-upon name of their own at the time "The Movement" first began gathering strength and making itself heard in the land. The values and ideals that underlay "The Movement" were nothing new to these shores: they had had their proponents and advocates in American public life for at least two centuries; they had even played an important part in the fomenting of the American Revolution. But their actual influence on American public opinion and public policy had declined steadily ever since the days of the Founding Fathers. Thus, in the early 1960s, when a new generation of young people, the cutting edge of the baby boom generation, began entering college and breathing new life and new power into these once venerable values and ideals, the names by which they had once been widely known—Individualist, Classical Liberal, Libertarian—had fallen into disuse and been virtually forgotten.

Under these circumstances, it isn't really that difficult to understand why the mass media of the early 1960s might have jumped to the conclusion that "The Movement" was a project of the Left. For one thing, it obviously *wasn't* a project of the Right: "The Movement" opposed both the war and the draft, while the Right strongly favored both. And if a political movement didn't belong on the Right, where else could it belong but on the Left? After all, for generations, student political activists—like political activists generally in this country—had come in only two main varieties: they had been either Right or Left. What other alternatives were there? What other alternatives *could* there be?

The answer to this question will depend, in large measure, on how you define the key terms "Left" and "Right." One way of formulating the difference between the two—a way which has steadily grown in popularity among political scientists in recent years—is to say that the Left advocates extensive government regulation of the individual's behavior in the economic sphere, but only minimal regulation of the individual's behavior in his or her personal life, while the Right advocates only minimal regulation of economic behavior but extensive regulation of personal behavior.

Thus the Left favors laws controlling prices, wages, rents, the hiring and firing policies of companies, and the distribution of wealth through the population, but opposes laws controlling entertainment and personal expression—the books and other publications we choose to read or look at, the plays or films or videos we choose to watch, the games we choose to play, the ways we choose to have sex, the things we choose to eat or drink or smoke or snort or inject into our bodies, and all the kinds of things we choose to create and place before the public as expressions of our own ideas, our own insights, our own personal and unique vision of "the way the world is."

Thus the Right opposes laws controlling the way individuals run the businesses they own—the prices and rents they charge, the wages they pay, their employment policies, and so forth—but favors laws controlling "pornography," "obscenity," "gambling," "drug abuse," and a variety of sexual practices, ranging from heterosexual prostitution to homosexual intercourse.

If this is the essence of the difference between Left and Right in American politics, it seems obvious that there are at least two alternative positions available to the political activist. On the one hand, a person could advocate extensive government regulation of *both* economic and personal behavior. Or one could advocate only minimal government regulation in both spheres of human activity.

Political scientists call the first of these alternatives the *Populist alternative*. The second they call the *Libertarian alternative*.

Let me say this in a slightly different way. All four of the factions that make modern American political reality what it is—the Left, the Right, the Populists, and the Libertarians—agree on one point: that the only legitimate purpose of any government is to build a better society for its citizens—to make it easier for its citizens to enjoy the many potential benefits of social living, while minimizing the likelihood that they will succumb to any of the various dangers which also seem built into the very process of living and working in close proximity to others of one's species.

The Left believes government can best achieve these goals by regulating its citizens' economic activities, while leaving them to make their own choices about how they conduct their personal lives.

The Right believes government can best fulfill its mandate by regulating its citizens' private lives, while leaving them free to do pretty much as they like in their economic activities.

The Populists believe government is best equipped to do its job when it regulates *both* the private and the economic behavior of its citizens.

The Libertarians believe that "that government is best which governs least"—that all of us have not only a much better chance of benefiting but also a significantly smaller chance of suffering from our close, daily interaction with each other when our government leaves us entirely—or almost entirely—to our own devices, both in our economic dealings and in our personal lives.

4

Anarchists and Minarchists

Before the early '60s, when the oldest baby boomers began arriving on college and university campuses nationwide, virtually all political activists had been either from the Left or from the Right. Then suddenly, beginning around 1963 or 1964, this changed. *Most* student political activists still seemed to come either from the Left or from the Right, but now, all at once, a substantial number of them—a number much too big to ignore—were neither Left nor Right but Libertarian.

Libertarians are of two sorts: there are the *anarchists* and there are the *minarchists*.[2] There are the advocates of no government at all, and there are the advocates of strictly limited government—the "night watchman state."

Neither of these doctrines was really either new or revolutionary when they began turning up on American college and university campuses back in the early 1960s. By that time, both of them had been expounded for some two hundred years in this country alone—and not just by a handful of obscure, utopian cranks and crackpots, either; rather, by some of the most respected and influential figures in all of American intellectual history. And the broader tradition of political philosophy from which they both derived was already far, far older at that time than the mere couple of centuries during which it had taken root and flourished on these shores. For, of course, neither anarchism nor classical liberalism (as minarchism or limited government libertarianism used to be called) is an American invention.

Historians of anarchist thought customarily trace its origins back to the ancient Chinese writings of Lao-tse. And historians of classical liberalism customarily locate the beginnings of that doctrine in the *Two Treatises of Government* published late in the seventeenth century by the English philosopher John Locke.

For many readers, the claim that these two strands of political thought are (and always have been) closely related will doubtless seem counterintuitive, if not utterly absurd. As one contemporary political scientist put it nearly fifteen years ago, in a tone of evident wonder: "The words 'anarchism' and '[classical] liberalism' do not usually occur together."

It seems evident, however, that the widespread belief in the fundamental incompatibility of anarchism and classical liberalism is due mainly to the stubborn persistence in the popular mind (and, alas, to a great extent also in the educated mind) of certain utterly baseless myths concerning anarchist theory.

The first of these is the myth that anarchists advocate violence—including not only the murder of government officials but also the bombing of public places and similar acts of terrorism against members of the general public. A second, and closely related myth holds that anarchists advocate an overall condition of disorder—even chaos—in society, as somehow preferable to a condition of peace and harmony.

With respect to both these myths, the actual truth of the matter is quite the opposite. Assassinations and terrorist attacks have been committed by self-proclaimed anarchists, to be sure—

just as they have been committed by self-proclaimed Christians, Moslems, monarchists, communists, and environmentalists. But, as George Woodcock, one of the best-known and fairest-minded of anarchism's historians, has put it, "at no time was a policy of terrorism adopted by anarchists in general."

Indeed, how could it have been? As another historian of anarchist thought, William O. Reichert, has pointed out, "rejection of force is fundamental to the thinking of all anarchists, and is the essential foundation of anarchism's entire philosophical structure."[3] It is much easier to think of anarchists (Leo Tolstoy, Dorothy Day, and Robert LeFevre spring immediately to mind) who have been led by their political ideals to advocate a thoroughgoing pacifism—rejecting all violence, even for purposes of self-defense—than it is to think of anarchists whose political ideals have led them to initiate force against others.

And as for the charge of advocating disorder and chaos, on the contrary: from the beginning, anarchists have believed that it is government which creates most social friction and disharmony, by attempting to force square individuals into round holes, by trying to coerce people and communities into procrustean beds made by law, and by setting Peter against Paul by robbing (i.e., taxing) the former in order to pay special favors to the latter. As Pierre Joseph Proudhon, the first writer ever to call himself an anarchist, put it in the middle of the last century, "liberty is the mother, not the daughter, of order."

Yet another baseless myth concerning anarchism is that its exponents are unalterably opposed to private property and to the unfettered operation of the free market. Not so. From the beginning, anarchists have been divided in their economic views. Some have been communists—that is, advocates of communal ownership of land and the other major means of production—while others have been unabashed partisans of individual property ownership and laissez-faire. More important, both the anarcho-communists and the anarcho-capitalists have been economic voluntarists. Neither side has advocated the use of coercion, the force of law, the power of government, to *require* compliance with its particular vision of the economically just society.

The case of the contemporary anarcho-communist Murray Bookchin is instructive in this connection. Asked in a 1978 interview how he would feel if the people of a particular town or region in an anarchist society chose voluntarily to establish a system of private property and market capitalism among themselves, Bookchin replied that though he considered that such a system would be immoral and unjust, he would vigorously oppose any attempt by his anarcho-communist colleagues to force the rebels to abandon their newly founded free-market system. Moreover, he said, if his fellow anarcho-communists actually attempted to coerce the anarcho-capitalists to return to the straight and narrow path, he would move to the anarcho-capitalist community and personally take up arms, if necessary, in their defense. To Bookchin, as to any true anarchist, economics is secondary; what is primary, what matters most, is that the individual, *every* individual, be free to go his or her own way, without fear of the organized power of others being turned against them as a result.

Seen in this way, stripped of the mythology that normally surrounds it, anarchism may be seen as it actually is: an extraordinarily close philosophical comrade-in-spirit of classical liberalism. As the contemporary political scientist Stephen L. Newman put it in 1984,

> [h]aving defined liberty as the absence of coercion and finding the exercise of political power to be a primary instance of coercion, [anarchists] logically conclude that liberty and government are incompatible. Defenders of the minimal state differ only in asserting that a small degree of personal liberty must be surrendered to government in exchange for the guaranteed security of life and property.[4]

As I have noted, neither of these doctrines, neither anarchism nor classical liberalism, was an American invention. But both of them found extraordinarily fertile ground for growth in the politically tumultuous America of the last decades of the eighteenth century.

5

The American Libertarian Tradition

The American "Founding Fathers"—the philosophers, polemicists, and men of affairs who prepared the way for the American Revolution, ran that Revolution once it had come into being, saw it through to its successful conclusion, and established the new government that replaced the ousted British colonial regime—were among the first and decidedly among the most successful political activists up to that time ever to employ the theory and rhetoric of classical liberalism as the basis for a popular rebellion against an established government. In part, their success was a function of the colonial population they were addressing. A substantial proportion of the rabble they were bent on rousing had come to America in the first place in order to escape what they regarded as the intolerably intrusive and coercive policies they had suffered under at home, in Great Britain. They had come to America in search of greater individual liberty. They had come here in search of a society in which they would be allowed greater freedom of action, greater personal autonomy, greater

31

personal control over their lives than they had ever been able to find for themselves at home.

When these men argued, as Thomas Jefferson, perhaps their most eloquent spokesman, did, that "that government is best which governs least," when they maintained that the only sort of government with any plausible claim to legitimacy is the kind of government that governs only by the authority and to the extent of the consent of those it governs, when they insisted that any truly legitimate government must confine itself strictly to protecting the "Natural Rights" of its citizens to "life, liberty, and the pursuit of happiness," they found plenty of willing listeners. And when, after the success of their War of Independence against England, these same men set about organizing a new government which had no power to tax and virtually no authority to regulate either the economic or the personal affairs of its citizens, one which was empowered to do little more than adjudicate certain disputes and provide for the national defense in the event of a direct attack from abroad (even such "basic" services as police protection against violent criminals being left entirely up to local authorities), again their efforts met with widespread popular acclaim. For the kind of national government the Founding Fathers authorized in the Articles of Confederation was much more to the liking of most Americans of that day than the kind of government they had long endured at the hands of the British crown.

Yet no sooner had the Founding Fathers finished founding and fathering this scrupulously limited, classically liberal government than various philosophical gadflies began taking intellectual potshots at their handiwork.

Far and away the most important of these early critics was Thomas Paine, whose genius as a propagandist and pamphleteer had, only a few years earlier, won him the status of a full-fledged Founding Father in his own right. Paine was perhaps the first in what was to become a long line of American political thinkers who, in William Reichert's words, "thought out for themselves the full social and philosophical implications of the concept of freedom . . . that is fundamental to this country."[5]

Social order, as Paine saw it,

> is not the effect of government. It has its origin in the principles of society and the natural constitution of men. It existed prior to government and would exist if the formality of government was abolished. The mutual dependence and reciprocal interest which man has upon man, and all the parts of civilized community upon each other, create that great chain of connection which holds it together. The landholder, the farmer, the manufacturer, the merchant, the tradesman, and every occupation, prospers by the aid which each receives from the other, and from the whole. Common interest regulates their concerns and forms their law; and the laws which common usage ordains, have a greater influence than the laws of government.

Indeed, according to Paine, government serves mainly as a hindrance to "the natural propensity to society" described in the preceding passage. He worked out his ideas on these and related matters between 1789 and 1792 in a series of lengthy and intellectually vigorous conversations with the British novelist, utopian, iconoclast, freethinker, and nonconformist William Godwin, who is perhaps best known today as the husband of the pioneer feminist Mary Wollstonecraft, and as the father of Mary Shelley (whose innovative first novel, *Frankenstein,* entitles her to a secure position of her own as a pioneer of a different sort— as one of the creators of modern science fiction).

Two books issued from this series of discussions between Paine and Godwin: Paine's *The Rights of Man* (1792), and Godwin's *An Enquiry Concerning Political Justice and Its Influence Upon General Virtue and Happiness* (1793).

In his *Enquiry,* Godwin took Paine's ideas even farther than Paine himself had taken them. Where Paine had grudgingly acknowledged that "government even in its best state is but a necessary evil," Godwin argued that even the most limited of governments, even the sort of government that is "intended to suppress injustice" and nothing more, must end up instead creating "new occasions and temptations for the commission" of injustice.

If our goal is to safeguard each individual's right to life, liberty, and the pursuit of happiness, Godwin reasoned, the very last thing we should consider doing to achieve this goal is creating an institution like government. For in order to be capable of protecting individual rights against both domestic criminals and foreign invaders, a government must be extraordinarily powerful. Yet any institution with that much power at its disposal has the potential, for that very reason, to become an even greater violator of individual rights than any of those against whom we are looking to it for protection. In effect, Godwin became the first political thinker to pose the question: who will protect us from our protectors?

This debate between the minarchists and the anarchists has continued ever since. And while political thinkers from other parts of the world have joined in the fray from time to time— Pierre Joseph Proudhon and Frederic Bastiat from France; Max Stirner and Rudolf Rocker from Germany; John Stuart Mill and Herbert Spencer from England; Michael Bakunin, Peter Kropotkin, and Leo Tolstoy from Russia; Mohandas Gandhi from India, to mention only a few of the more obvious examples—this debate has been primarily American. More of the participants in the controversy have come from the United States than from any other nation. Indeed, more of the participants have come from the United States than from all other nations combined.

Nor is this fact to be wondered at. Of all the nations of the modern world, the one whose political culture is most explicitly based in a reverential respect for individual liberty and a systemic distrust of and determination to severely restrict governmental authority is the United States. As William O. Reichert puts it, both anarchism and the "classical liberal" minarchism from which it derives are "as 'American' in character as the Fourth of July."[6]

Hardly had the nineteenth century dawned in America before its leading intellectual lights were hurling themselves with a vengeance into the ongoing debate over the legitimacy of government authority over the individual. In Concord, New Hampshire, Ralph Waldo Emerson was observing that "the less government we have the better," that "good men must not obey the laws too well," and that "the best citizens are not the 'law-abiding' ones, but rather they who by breaking laws, make way for progress." At the same time, Emerson's close friend and confidant, Bronson Alcott, father of the later much-celebrated children's author Louisa May Alcott, was demanding to know "Why should I hire a state to govern me? Why not govern myself?" And Henry David Thoreau, whose place in literary and intellectual history has ultimately come to seem even more secure than Emerson's or Alcott's—Thoreau, who can now lay better claim to permanent, "classic" status than any of the other illustrious members of that Concord circle—Thoreau was busily following his lifelong habit of expressing himself even more bluntly than even the most plainspoken and direct of his contemporaries: "I heartily accept the motto,—'That government is best which governs least,'" Thoreau wrote in 1848,

> and I should like to see it acted up to more rapidly and systematically. Carried out it finally amounts to this, which I also believe,— "That government is best which governs not at all," and when men are prepared for it, that will be the kind of government which they will have.[7]

Meanwhile, dozens of less widely known American political philosophers and radical activists were energetically pursuing their own ideas and ideals and arriving at remarkably similar conclusions. There was Josiah Warren, for example, the founder of several experimental governmentless communities (one of which, Long Island's Modern Times, turned out to be the longest lived of all the many and infinitely varied attempts to realize Utopia in the "virgin wilderness" of nineteenth-century America).

There was Stephen Pearl Andrews, who debated free love and political liberty with Henry James and Horace Greeley in the pages of the *New York Tribune* and preached in his *magnum opus The Science of Society* (1851) that "diversity reigns throughout every kingdom of nature" and "mocks at all attempts to make laws, or constitutions, or regulations of any sort, which shall work justly and harmoniously amidst the unforeseen contingencies of the future."

There was Lysander Spooner, the lawyer and polemicist who first attracted wide public attention during the days of the abolitionist movement, then turned his attention to denouncing government as such in no uncertain terms, as nothing more than a more highly organized and more impertinent version of that long familiar evil, highway robbery. "The highwayman," Spooner wrote in 1870,

does not pretend that he has any rightful claim to your money, or that he intends to use it for your own benefit. He does not pretend to be anything but a robber. He has not acquired impudence enough to profess to be merely a "protector," and that he takes men's money against their will, merely to enable him to "protect" those infatuated travellers, who feel perfectly able to protect themselves, or do not appreciate his peculiar system of protection. He is too sensible a man to make such professions as these. Furthermore, having taken your money, he leaves you, as you wish him to do. He does not persist in following you on the road, against your will; assuming to be your rightful "sovereign," on account of the "protection" he affords you. He does not keep "protecting" you, by commanding you to bow down and serve him; by requiring you to do this, and forbidding you to do that; by robbing you of more money as often as he finds it for his interest or pleasure to do so; and by branding you as a rebel, a traitor, and an enemy to your country, and shooting you down without mercy, if you dispute his authority, or resist his demands. He is too much of a gentleman to be guilty of such impostures, and insults, and villainies as these. In short, he does not, in addition to robbing you, attempt to make you either his dupe or his slave.[8]

There was Benjamin R. Tucker, the Boston printer, journalist, and bookseller who described himself interchangeably as an "anarchist" and as an "unterrified Jeffersonian democrat" (he maintained that the two were one and the same thing). *Liberty,* the weekly paper Tucker edited from 1881 to 1908, attracted thousands of subscribers from all over the English-speaking (and English-reading) world and counted such literary heavyweights as George Bernard Shaw among its contributors.

Meanwhile, American minarchists were by no means holding either their tongues or their peace. At Yale, for example, the pioneer sociologist William Graham Sumner was extolling the virtues of strictly limited "constitutional government," as the only effective means to "prevent the abusive control" of society by its strongest and most powerful members. And the most widely influential American political movement of the nineteenth century, the "Single Tax" movement, was based on the teachings of Henry George, who argued that progress could be virtually guaranteed and poverty virtually abolished if only men could be made to see the wisdom of setting up a government so decidedly minimalist that it did hardly anything at all besides assessing and collecting a "Single Tax," to be paid by landlords.

The early years of the twentieth century are best known to historians of American political thought for the enormous growth they witnessed in the prestige and popularity of *less* limited government. But while the ideas of those social theorists who advocated an increase in government power, especially those who styled themselves socialists or progressives, did begin to assume a new and (for this country) unprecedented importance during these years, the old, traditional debate between the anarchist and minarchist libertarians continued through this troubled time as well.

As in the past, the debate was not confined to the works of political philosophers and other similarly systematic social thinkers and scholars. An important role was also played by critics, essayists, and practitioners of what used to be called "the higher journalism." Ambrose Bierce defined "politics" in his *Devil's Dictionary* as "a strife of interests masquerading as a contest of principles," and "the conduct of public affairs for private advantage."[9]

James Gibbons Huneker, probably the leading American magazine essayist of the early twentieth century, introduced his American readers to European writers like Max Stirner, who asserted in his best-known book *The Ego and His Own* that "the State calls its own violence law, but that of the individual crime."

Among the most prominent of the younger American magazinists who began to attract attention during the second and third decades of this century, were Randolph "War Is the Health of the State" Bourne, who wavered philosophically between anarchism and minarchism, while consistently warning his readers to be on guard against what he believed was every government's never-ending effort to use war as a means and pretext for expanding its power over the individual; Albert Jay Nock, a former Single Taxer whose book *Our Enemy, the State* (1934) is perhaps the best single book ever written by an American libertarian; and H. L. Mencken, who claimed to be "a libertarian of the most extreme variety," a man who was "against jailing men for their opinions, or, for that matter, for anything else," a man who thought the ideal government would be "one which barely escapes being no government at all." By the mid-1920s, Mencken was being called (by the *New York Times)* "the most powerful private citizen in America" and (by Walter Lippman in the *New York Herald-Tribune*) "the greatest single influence on this entire generation of educated people."

There were also libertarian political activists on the American scene during this period, of course. One of them, Emma Goldman, made herself into perhaps the single most influential communist anarchist in the world, and used her influence to warn her fellow anarcho-communists against confusing the so-called Noble Experiment being conducted by the Bolshevik regime in Russia at that time with true—that is, voluntary and stateless—communism. Later, during the 1930s, still another purely voluntary native American anarcho-communist movement, the Catholic Worker movement, "arose" or "emerged" or whatever other verb might seem somehow more appropriate, under the leadership of Dorothy Day and Ammon Hennacy.

After the 1930s, however, exponents of the libertarian point of view became steadily fewer and farther between in both American publishing and American politics. And this was to have unexpected and far-reaching consequences a few more decades down the line.

6

Origins of the Modern Libertarian Movement

During the fall semester of 1964, when the oldest members of the baby boom generation first began enrolling for classes at colleges and universities nationwide, there were far more libertarians among them, whether anarchist or minarchist, than there had been in any previous generation of students within living memory. But the budding writers and political activists among these libertarians found no already existing libertarian student organizations into which they could channel their ideas and their prodigious energy. Instead they found two already long established nonlibertarian national student political organizations waiting to take them in.

The first of these organizations was YAF (pronounced to rhyme with "staff")—Young Americans for Freedom—a group founded in 1960 on the grounds of William F. Buckley Jr.'s estate in Sharon, Connecticut. YAF, like the fortnightly conservative magazine, the *National Review* (*NR*), was sustained by Buckley's personal fortune. Like *NR,* YAF relied on Buckley to

41

guarantee its ongoing vitality and viability in the face of widespread and steadily growing hostility to certain of its official policies—most notably its support for U.S. involvement in the Vietnam War—which might otherwise so limit its ability to attract adequate voluntary financial support from students as to compromise its continued existence.

The second nationwide student political organization the oldest of the baby boomers found already in place and waiting for them when they arrived on campus in the mid-1960s was SDS—Students for a Democratic Society.

SDS was "founded" in 1960 as well, when an earlier group called the Student League for Industrial Democracy, "child of the venerable League for Industrial Democracy," as Milton Viorst writes, "whose Socialist origins dated back to such radical luminaries as Jack London and Upton Sinclair early in the century," repackaged itself with a $10,000 grant from the United Auto Workers and changed its name to Students for a Democratic Society.[10] Unlike YAF, which was pretty much devoted by its charter to the policies of the conservative wing of the Republican Party (the policies which had typified Barry Goldwater's campaign for the presidency in 1964), SDS was looser and had more ideological latitude from the beginning. Of course, SDS was conceived from the beginning (by its underwriters, at least) as an organization that would work to advance the interests of "the worker," as those interests had traditionally been conceived by the Left—strong unions; government-guaranteed or government-provided health care, education, and retirement; and so forth.

But the dominant theme in the SDS charter itself was a commitment to the ideal of "participatory democracy." From the beginning, that is, SDS was supposed to be mainly committed—committed above all else—to making it possible for each and every individual (i.e., each and every "worker") to use the *vote* to advance his or her interests, whatever those interests might be. So it is, for example, that, as the years went by, SDS came increasingly to argue against U.S. involvement in the Vietnam War on the grounds that, by participating in the war, the U.S. government was undermining the sacred right of the Vietnamese people to democratically choose a communist government for themselves. And so it is that SDS "cofounder" Tom Hayden has based his political career since the '60s largely on the doctrine of "economic democracy"—the idea that people have a right to "participate" by voting in the "economic decisions that affect their lives."

In any previous generation, if politically concerned students had come to college and found two already established organizations already there waiting for them, one dedicated to the goals and ideals of the Right, the other dedicated to the goals and ideals of the Left, this would have been sufficient.

But for many of the politically concerned students of the baby boom generation this was *not* sufficient. Too many of the politically concerned students of *this* generation were neither on the Right nor on the Left; too many of them had abandoned both the Right and the Left for one version or another of libertarianism.

On a few campuses, the libertarian political activists were numerous enough to form their own organizations—for example, at the University of Wisconsin at Madison, and at the University of California at Berkeley, where the newly founded Alliance of Libertarian Activists played a key role in launching the famous Free Speech Movement of 1964.

But most of the libertarian-leaning students who wanted to become politically active during the early-to-mid 1960s had to settle for less—by fitting themselves as best they could, like square pegs into round holes, into either YAF or SDS.

Those who chose YAF and later gathered together to form a Libertarian Caucus within that conservative organization were mostly former conservatives—former partisans of the Right—themselves, young people who had come to their libertarian views under the influence of such older onetime conservatives as Leonard Read, Robert LeFevre, and Karl Hess.

In the late 1940s, Read, a former president of the Los Angeles Chamber of Commerce and author of the book *Anything That's Peaceful,* had become CEO of a newly founded nonprofit, tax-exempt "think tank" called the Foundation for Economic Education (FEE). Under his leadership FEE began publishing books, pamphlets, and a monthly magazine called the *Freeman,* sponsoring essay contests and two-week summer seminars in political economy for college students, and supplying thick files of clippings on each year's national high school debate topic, free of charge, to high school debaters all over the country. FEE reached untold thousands of young people in these ways during the first decade and a half of its existence. By the late 1950s and early 1960s, it had become unquestionably the most powerful and influential institutional advocate of limited government libertarianism in the world.

FEE's closest competitor at the time was probably the Freedom School (later Rampart College), an explicitly libertarian institution of higher learning founded in the mid-1950s by a former actor, broadcaster, real-estate salesman, and unsuccessful Republican congressional candidate named Robert LeFevre.

LeFevre had spent the last few years just before he decided to launch the Freedom School in the newspaper business, mainly as a columnist and editorial writer in the employ of an eccentric newspaper publisher named R. C. Hoiles. Hoiles believed in private property, free enterprise, and self-government. He believed that each individual should govern himself or herself, and no one else. Hoiles contended that no government could legitimately take any action which would be improper or immoral or unjust if it were undertaken by an individual.

Hoiles reasoned, for example, that if it is theft for an individual to take the property of someone else without consent, then it is theft for government to do the same thing; he concluded, therefore, that government has no right to collect taxes or to exercise the power of eminent domain. As Hoiles saw it, if it was wrong for an individual to use the threat of force in order to insure that others followed certain rules in their conduct of their private lives and their business affairs, then it was wrong for government to ban or regulate such behavior as gambling, drug use, and the sale of sexual favors, and it was equally wrong for government to regulate commerce by means of licensing laws, zoning laws, building codes, and other such devices; if it was wrong for an individual to enslave a person, even for a short time, then it was equally wrong for government to force any individual to perform military service or to appear in a courtroom (or anywhere else) or to engage in any involuntary speaking or writing of any kind—as government regularly does when it compels testimony in certain legal proceedings and when it requires that individuals answer certain questions and provide certain information if ordered to do so by police officers and/or various other government officials.

For R. C. Hoiles, government had no business running schools or delivering mail or building hospitals or parks or even roads. As far as Hoiles was concerned, the only legitimate activities of government were those which would also be legitimate if engaged in by individuals—like fighting back against aggressors. And even that would be improper, Hoiles felt, if government stole (i.e., imposed taxes to raise) the money it needed to finance its efforts against criminals and foreign invaders.

Every paper Hoiles owned expounded this libertarian philosophy on its editorial page. And after a few years of expounding it himself in the editorials he wrote every day for the *Gazette-Telegraph,* the Hoiles paper in Colorado Springs, Robert LeFevre found that he'd persuaded himself to abandon the conservative views he'd once believed in. He found he'd shifted his allegiance to a libertarian viewpoint instead. He also found that in the process of becoming a libertarian he'd lost much of his former interest in the newspaper business and conceived a new desire to devote himself instead to teaching and the writing of books.

He opened his Freedom School in June 1956 on a rustic, picturesque campus in the foothills of the Rockies, about halfway between Denver and Colorado Springs, just outside the tiny village of Larkspur, Colorado. And the books he had decided he wanted to write began to appear not long afterward: *The Nature of Man and His Government, The Philosophy of Ownership, This Bread Is Mine,* and all the others.

Meanwhile, another former journalist, Karl Hess, who had worked as a writer and editor for major national publications like *Newsweek* throughout the 1950s, had begun directing his considerable rhetorical talents in a more explicitly political direction. By 1964 he was writing speeches for Barry Goldwater, that year's GOP presidential candidate, putting into the Arizona senator's mouth such famous phrases as the declarations that "extremism in defense of liberty is no vice" and that "moderation in opposition to tyranny is no virtue." By 1969, Hess was extolling "The Death of Politics" in a major essay in *Playboy* magazine—extolling, that is, what he saw as a growing movement away from politics as such, away from any sort of belief in the usefulness of government as a means of solving social problems, and toward a broadly "libertarian" ethic which emphasized self-reliance, self-help, and voluntary, mostly ad hoc, cooperative efforts among the members of individual neighborhoods and communities. And by 1966, Hess had joined Murray Rothbard as coeditor of a monthly newsletter called the *Libertarian Forum.*

Rothbard was a maverick economist, an exponent of something called "Austrian Economics," which, back in the mid-1960s, was so obscure that it was almost impossible to find even a professional economist who had ever heard of it. And those you could find back then, even among the ranks of professional economists, could probably have been counted, as Vladimir Nabokov says, on the fingers of one deformed hand.

The Austrian School of Economics had been founded nearly a hundred years earlier, in the 1870s, in Austria, by one Carl

Menger. "Menger's ideas," according to political scientist Stephen L. Newman, "were developed and promulgated by his students Eugen von Böhm-Bawerk and Friedrich von Wieser at the University of Vienna. Their work was carried on in Vienna and later in America by Ludwig von Mises."[11] *Human Action: A Treatise on Economics* (1948), the largest and most philosophically dense of Mises's many books, is now generally regarded as the bible of Austrianism.

Of Mises's own students, the three who have most distinguished themselves have been Friedrich A. von Hayek (winner of the Nobel Prize in economics in 1974, by which time Austrianism had obviously already succeeded in becoming considerably less obscure), Israel Kirzner, and Murray Rothbard.

During the three centuries or so during which economics has been formally studied and theorized about in the West, it has been common for those doing the studying and theorizing, particularly for those economists whose natural inclination is toward a broadly philosophical outlook on human affairs generally, to reason their way from whatever theory of economics they have decided to adopt to some compatible theory of politics and government. Indeed, not a few economists have aimed from the beginning at nothing less than this. As the title of his magnum opus, *Human Action,* suggests, for example, Ludwig von Mises intended all along to formulate not merely a theory of economics, but a theory of human social interaction.

Like his Austrian predecessors, and like his most illustrious pupil, Friedrich A. von Hayek, Mises coupled his devotion to laissez-faire and his commitment to the free market with an allegiance to classical liberalism, which is to say, minarchism or "limited government libertarianism." Murray Rothbard was the first prominent Austrian economist to find his way from Austrianism to anarchism instead.

He was also the first Austrian to seek common cause with the American Left. Since shortly after he first took up residence in this country, Rothbard's teacher, Mises, had associated himself primarily with the Right. By 1968, with his full knowledge and consent, his books had been peddled aggressively for two decades by various American conservative publishers, booksellers, and activist groups. Thousands of copies of *Human Action,* an extraordinarily abstract and difficult work, one of the most intellectually challenging books of its kind ever published in this country, had been distributed throughout the 1950s and 1960s by the right-wing Conservative Book Club, an organization whose usual fare ran more toward simplistic tracts against the evils of "godless communism" and rock 'n' roll music.

By contrast, as early as 1965, Rothbard had begun writing about the many important ways in which libertarians and the so-called New Left—i.e., SDS—stood on common ground. He described SDS's early years as exemplifying "a striking and splendid infusion of libertarianism into the ranks of the Left," and approvingly quoted a student activist who proclaimed that the New Left had "taken up a 'right wing' cause which the avowed conservatives have dropped in favor of defending corporations and hunting Communists. This is the cause of the individual against the world."[12] By 1968, Rothbard had taken his call for a New Left/libertarian alliance to the pages of *Ramparts,* then the premier New Left journal of opinion.

The conventional wisdom of the 1990s would seem to suggest that when Rothbard thought he saw a distinctly libertarian strain in the New Left of the mid-1960s, he was only deceiving himself in an orgy of wishful thinking. Rothbard himself later recanted and renounced the views he had expressed in the passages quoted above, and allied himself with the Right.

But in fact, at the time, Rothbard was *not* being fanciful. On the contrary, he was exhibiting a clearer vision and a fuller understanding of what was actually going on around him than any other contemporary analyst of political trends among the young.

For just as there were libertarians who were trying to fit themselves into YAF during the mid-1960s, so there were other libertarians who were trying to fit themselves into SDS. Carl Oglesby,
who was president of SDS during 1965 and 1966, has described
the original New Left as an alliance of "true progressives, classical
liberals, humanistic revolutionaries, and libertarians."[13]

The chief difference between the young libertarians who
chose to join SDS back in the mid-1960s and the young libertarians who chose to join YAF during that same period was in the
intellectual influences that had shaped their political thinking.
The YAF libertarians had followed the lead of men like Read,
Hoiles, LeFevre, Hess, and Rothbard, men who had started out
as advocates of free-market economics and found their way to
libertarianism by pursuing the wider implications of economic
laissez-faire to their logical conclusions. The SDS libertarians
had followed the lead of theorists of a different sort, writers like
Paul Goodman and Jane Jacobs, writers who would be joined
shortly, in the late 1960s, by an articulate newcomer called
Murray Bookchin. These were writers who had started out, not
with an economic theory, but with a more broadly social theory,
a vision of the fundamental nature of human society as such.

Those who shared this vision looked at human society and
the various folkways and institutions that enabled any particular
human society to hold together and endure over time, and what
they saw were the workings of natural processes, literally forces
of nature—processes of essentially the same kind as the ones
which hold an ecosystem together and enable it to endure over
time. To these left libertarians, the idea of *governing* human
social relations through the use of force is as futile and as dangerous as the idea of taking over and controlling the life within a
rain forest or across a prairie or along the shoreline of a moun-
tain stream. "For both the ecologist and the anarchist," William
O. Reichert writes in a discussion of the ideas of Murray
Bookchin,

> the most striking characteristic of nature is the spontaneity that lies at the bottom of every natural growth pattern. Natural living processes atrophy and die to the extent that they are artificially restricted and caged within imposed regimens of force and restraint.[14]

This conception of human society turns up not only in Bookchin's writings, but also in Paul Goodman's impassioned defenses, in books like *Growing Up Absurd* (1960) and *Compulsory Mis-education* (1964), of the need for spontaneity and creative individual freedom in the learning process. It turns up too in Jane Jacobs's famous, pathbreaking portrayals of the unregulated, unplanned city as the natural, virtually organic form which human society takes when it is allowed to develop on its own, ungoverned, and in her insistence that the nation, by contrast, is an unnatural and essentially antisocial institution which has been imposed upon men by force.

Of course this very same "ecological" conception of what might well be termed the *natural law* of human social relations is also to be found in the writings of various political and economic theorists more beloved of the American political Right of the mid-1960s than of the American political Left. It is the conception Adam Smith was attempting to describe back in 1776 in *The Wealth of Nations,* when he wrote of the "invisible hand" that seemed to coordinate and bring a kind of order to what one might well expect would be instead the utter chaos of a totally free, utterly unregulated marketplace. It is the conception the Austrian economist Friedrich von Hayek was attempting to formulate when he argued that there is a "spontaneous order," an order which is "the product of human action but not of human design," and which is the natural order of human society, with which rulers and planners tinker at their peril.

How could it be otherwise? For in the end, whatever variety of libertarian thought we examine, we will always find ourselves back at the same basic philosophical foundation.

Because this foundation is fundamentally neither of the Left nor of the Right, however, the libertarian political activists of the mid-1960s who attempted to make homes for themselves in organizations like SDS and YAF discovered before very long that this approach could work, if at all, only in the very short term. Philosophical differences led inevitably to differences on issues, on strategy, and on tactics; and these differences led to factional fights for organizational control. By 1969, most of the libertarians had been purged from SDS. In that same year, the entire membership of the Libertarian Caucus was purged from YAF at that organization's national convention.

Meanwhile, a related development of extraordinary importance had occurred: the collapse late in 1968 of the Objectivist movement, which had grown up around the passionate, intellectually exhilarating writings (and, to an extent, the flamboyantly charismatic personality) of one of the central figures in the youth rebellion of the '60s—the controversial novelist, philosopher, and polemicist, Ayn Rand.

7

Who Was Ayn Rand?

Rand was born Alicia Rosenbaum in St. Petersburg (Leningrad), Russia, on February 2, 1905. She earned a degree in history and philosophy at the University of Leningrad, graduating in 1926. Shortly thereafter, she obtained permission from the Soviet government to visit for a few months with relatives in the United States. She never returned to Russia.

Instead, after spending only a short time in Chicago with her relatives, Rand moved on to Los Angeles, where she managed to earn a subsistence income in the film industry while teaching herself English, the language in which she had decided she would write the novels she had been planning to write for more than a decade. The first of her novels to see print, *We the Living,* a bitterly pessimistic tale of the Russian Revolution and its aftermath, was published by Macmillan in 1936. Rand adopted her now internationally famous pseudonym at this time in the hope that she might thereby protect the members of her family who were still living in Russia from

being punished for the "crime" of being related to such a virulently anti-Soviet writer.

During the next few years, Rand turned out a play, a courtroom drama called *The Night of January 16th,* which enjoyed a
modestly successful run on Broadway; she also found a British
publisher (but failed to find an American one) for a second novel,
Anthem, a short, poetic fantasy which depicted the successful
escape of a pair of lovers from a totalitarian state of the far
future.

Then, in 1943, at the age of thirty-eight, Rand published her
third novel, the one which was to prove her breakthrough success. *The Fountainhead,* the triumphant story of Howard Roark,
architect, genius, and intransigent individualist, sold well enough
in its first year of publication to show up here and there on the
bestseller lists without exactly qualifying as a true bestseller. And
where hardcover sales are concerned, most novels sell more
copies during their first year in print than they are ever able to
sell in any subsequent year. But *The Fountainhead* sold more
copies in 1944 than it did in 1943. Not only that, it sold more
copies in 1945 than it had in 1944. And so it went, year after
year, all the way up to 1952, when it first appeared in a paperback edition.

By this time, *The Fountainhead* had not only sold more than
400,000 hardcover copies, it had also spent a few more weeks on
the hardcover bestseller lists, where it staged an almost unprecedented reappearance in 1949, a full six years after its original
publication. (Presumably this reappearance was at least partly a
result of the publicity received by the 1949 release of the film
version of the novel, starring Gary Cooper, Patricia Neal, and
Raymond Massey.)

Rand's next, and biggest, bestseller came in 1957. *Atlas
Shrugged* is one of the few (and, at more than a thousand closely
printed pages, one of the longest) works of fiction ever written
which could be plausibly described both as a "thriller" and as a

"novel of ideas." Its elaborately intricate and ingeniously complex plot, part science fiction, part detective story, is unique in twentieth-century literature. Its highly stylized and theatrical—even operatic—characters are like those in no other novel anywhere. Its portrayal of the drama and excitement, the challenges and creativity of entrepreneurship and top-level management in the world of big business is unlike anything in the fiction of today or of any other time. It offers its readers an "unputdownable" story full of surprises and cliffhangers, but frequently interrupts the action to allow its characters to deliver highly abstract philosophical speeches of anywhere from around three pages to more than sixty pages in length.

The longest and most theoretical of these speeches is delivered late in the novel by its hero, John Galt, a physicist, engineer, and inventor who has deliberately brought about the collapse of civilization by leading a "strike of the men of the mind," having persuaded the creative geniuses whose achievements are the source of all civilization and progress to withdraw from the world and stop producing. Galt's speech serves a purely fictional or artistic purpose in the working out of the novel's plot, for Galt must make sure that those he has abandoned in a collapsing civilization are made to understand *why* their civilization is collapsing; otherwise he runs the risk that the point he wanted to make, the lesson he led his strike in order to teach, will be lost upon his students.

Galt's speech is more than a mere plot device, however. Rand meant it to serve also as a preliminary summary of what she said was "a new philosophical system" which she had devised and christened "Objectivism." She planned, she said, to give her "full system . . . a detailed, systematic presentation in a philosophical treatise."[15] But she never did. Aside from a brief monograph on her theory of concepts and perhaps a dozen essays on various issues in ethics, aesthetics, and political theory, Rand never produced any formal philosophical writing of any sort at all. Nor did she produce any more fiction. Instead, she devoted the last twenty-odd years of her career to polemical writing on current political, cultural, and artistic controversies. Every few years she gathered the most recent of these polemical pieces together into a book-length manuscript and issued an anthology. The first of these collections, *The Virtue of Selfishness,* appeared in 1964. The last of them, *Philosophy: Who Needs It?* appeared shortly after her death in 1982.

By that time, an Objectivist movement of some sort could still be said to exist, but it was a tiny and feeble thing, the merest shadow (if even that) of the original Objectivist movement that flourished during the 1960s.

The original Objectivist movement was launched early in 1958, a few months after *Atlas Shrugged* hit the top spot on every major bestseller list in the country. It was launched not by Rand herself, but by a young psychologist named Nathaniel Branden, who was not only Rand's chief disciple and protégé (she spoke of him publicly as her "intellectual heir"), but also, since 1955, her lover.

Branden, a man of genuine and remarkable intellectual gifts in his own right, also exhibited extraordinary talent as a writer, as a public speaker, as an entrepreneur, and as a manager. He wrote a series of twenty ninety-minute lectures on "The Basic Principles of Objectivism," in which he made an impressive beginning on the task Rand herself had promised to undertake but never ultimately got around to—the task of formulating and working out the implications of his mentor's ideas in the more or less "official" style employed at that time by most professional philosophers and with careful attention to all the prevailing professional standards any thinker was expected to observe if he wanted his work to be taken seriously (or even to have its existence publicly acknowledged) by anyone in the mainstream of professional philosophy. It is unfortunate that Branden's "Basic Principles" course has never been published in book form, for it remains the clearest and most systematic general introduction to Objectivism; it is literally indispensable to anyone seriously interested in learning what Objectivism the philosophical theory (as opposed to Objectivism the cult, Objectivism the intellectual movement, and Objectivism the diffuse, quasi-Nietzschean spirit or sense of life which permeates Rand's novels) is all about.

Having written his lectures, Branden then set about establishing an organization, the Nathaniel Branden Institute (NBI), under whose auspices he could (and did) advertise and deliver them. He persuaded Rand to launch and coedit with him a monthly periodical in which her ideas would be applied to current public issues. He published a book of his own, *Who Is Ayn Rand?* (1962), which incorporated material from his lectures and was obviously meant to call the existence (nay, the ready availability) of those lectures and the philosophy of Objectivism to the attention of a wider audience.

Meanwhile, Rand's novels—particularly *The Fountainhead* and *Atlas Shrugged*—were continuing to sell like the proverbial hotcakes—particularly to young readers. When *Atlas Shrugged* appeared in a mass-market paperback edition in 1963, it almost immediately became the nation's number-one mass-market paperback fiction bestseller. And for several years thereafter it was difficult to find a high school or college student anywhere in the country who was at all bookish in his or her tastes who wasn't reading *Atlas Shrugged* or hadn't read it already. The success of *Atlas Shrugged* also led to the publication of new hardcover and paperback editions of Rand's first two novels, *We the Living* and *Anthem*. These books promptly began selling like hotcakes themselves. Two other volumes issued by Rand during the early '60s—*For the New Intellectual* (1961), a collection of the philosophical speeches embedded in her four novels, together with a long title essay on the role philosophical ideas had played in Western history, and *The Virtue of Selfishness* (1964), her first collection of her philosophical and polemical essays—sold fewer copies than her reissued novels did. But they achieved a certain popularity of their own, nonetheless, especially on campus, and they led many thousands of intellectually oriented baby boomers into the Objectivist movement.

By 1965, *Newsweek* was able to report, in a cover story summarizing the results of a series of opinion polls the magazine had conducted on college campuses nationwide, that Ayn Rand was one of the names its pollsters heard most frequently when they asked students who their "heroes" were.

Thirteen years later, when a pair of young journalists, Rex Weiner and Deanne Stillman, teamed up with an independent pollster to conduct what they called the "Woodstock Census"— an exhaustive survey of former "sixties people" (people who had been students during that decade)—they asked their respondents a similar question: "Back in the '60s," they inquired, "who did you admire most and feel most influenced by?"

One respondent in six named Ayn Rand in response to this question. She came in twenty-ninth out of eighty-one. And if you eliminate the politicians and entertainers from the list in order to find out which *authors* the young people of the '60s admired most and felt most influenced by, you find Rand coming in tied for sixth place with Germaine Greer. Only Kurt Vonnegut, Kahlil Gibran, Tom Wolfe, Jean-Paul Sartre and Albert Camus (who tied for fourth), and Allen Ginsberg received more votes than the author of *The Fountainhead* and *Atlas Shrugged.*

Of course, most of the young people who read, admired, and felt influenced by Ayn Rand during the 1960s didn't, strictly speaking, become involved in the Objectivist movement: they didn't sign up for NBI lecture courses, subscribe to the *Objectivist Newsletter* or the *Objectivist,* join campus Ayn Rand clubs, and call themselves "Students of Objectivism." (*Students of Objectivism* was the term Rand mandated for her young admirers; in her view, only she herself, Nathaniel Branden, and a few of their closest friends and associates could rightly describe themselves as

Objectivists.) What the majority of the young people who read and admired Ayn Rand during the '60s mean when they say she influenced them is not that she influenced them to adopt certain specific theories or particular philosophical ideas, but rather that she influenced certain of their general attitudes.

For example, consider the attitude so many young people seemed to adopt toward the matter of age back in the '60s—their attitude toward how important it was how old a person was. Didn't they talk back then as though they considered the young to be uniquely qualified—qualified by the very tenderness of their years—to see through and expose the hypocrisies and other evils of their elders? Didn't they soberly counsel each other back then not to "trust anyone over thirty"?

Well, one place they could easily have picked up such an attitude was from the pages of *Atlas Shrugged.* For in *Atlas Shrugged,* all the major heroic characters are young or youthful—and the villains, when they aren't actually, chronologically, past the middle years of their lives, are almost all prematurely aged.

Thus Dagny Taggart, the novel's heroine, looks "like a young girl; only her mouth and eyes [show] that she [is] a woman in her thirties." Francisco d'Anconia, a "playboy" in his mid-thirties, is sitting on the floor of his hotel room when the reader of *Atlas Shrugged* first makes his acquaintance, playing marbles and smiling "the unchanged, insolent, brilliant smile of his childhood." And when Francisco looks at Hank Rearden, who is, at forty-five, the most elderly of the heroic characters in the novel, he sees "the eyes of youth looking at the future with no uncertainty or fear."

The villainous James Taggart, on the other hand, "looked like a man approaching fifty, who had crossed into age from adolescence, without the intermediate stage of youth," despite the fact that "he was thirty-nine years old." And Hank Rearden's evil brother Philip "was thirty-eight, but his chronic weakness made people think at times that he was older than his brother."

Were the young people of the '60s profoundly unimpressed
with the offerings of the colleges and universities in which most
of them were enrolled? So was the youthful Francisco d'Anconia
in *Atlas Shrugged.*

"They're teaching a lot of drivel nowadays," he tells Dagny
when she asks him about his classes at the Patrick Henry University of Cleveland. And when his father asks him why he
decided to start his own copper business while still a full-time
undergraduate, he replies, "I couldn't have stood four years of
nothing but lectures."

Were the young people of the '60s openly contemptuous of
establishment intellectuals, conventional wisdom, and eternal
verities? Well, *Atlas Shrugged* contains perhaps the most acid-
etched portrait of establishment intellectualdom ever published
in America. From Dr. Simon Pritchett to Dr. Floyd Ferris to the
novelist Balph Eubank to that paragon of what used to be called
"the higher journalism," Bertram Scudder, the American intellectual establishment as portrayed in *Atlas Shrugged* is nothing
but a collection of frauds, mountebanks, and outright jackasses,
entirely unworthy of the respect of any decent human being of
average intelligence. *Atlas Shrugged* stands all of contemporary
conventional wisdom on its head. And as far as eternal verities
are concerned, Ayn Rand herself never tired of remarking that
her big novel challenged the entire cultural tradition of the past
two thousand years of Western civilization.

Were the young people of the '60s inclined to believe that a
woman was as good as anybody else? Well, reading *Atlas
Shrugged* could have done nothing but fuel their fire with regard
to that attitude. For here was a deeply intellectual novel written
by a woman and depicting the adventures of one of the most
extraordinary woman characters to be found anywhere in twentieth-century fiction: a beautiful female entrepreneur who flies
her own plane, runs her own railroad, and takes her own risks,
while exhibiting equal skill at engineering, philosophy, tennis,

housework, and sex; a woman who is not only as good as any man but in fact better—far better than almost any man you'll ever meet, either in fiction or out of it.

Did the young people of the '60s hold a dim view of the "military-industrial complex"? Well, they certainly found nothing in *Atlas Shrugged* that would be likely to make them reconsider that attitude. In fact, if one were to judge the worlds of government, big business, and the scientific establishment purely on the basis of reading *Atlas Shrugged,* one would have to conclude that almost all big businessmen are parasitic incompetents who owe their profits to special deals worked out for them by politicians, that the scientific establishment is nothing but an arm of government, and that the principal function of government is to employ stolen resources in the invention of loathsome weapons of mass destruction.

The young people who not only read Rand's novels during the '60s but also went on to become involved in the Objectivist movement learned to think of government in a somewhat, but only slightly, different way. In her essays on political philosophy, in her polemical pieces on current issues, and in the lectures NBI offered, with her approval, on her theories of human social relations, Rand preached that government, which she defined sometimes as "an institution that holds the exclusive power to *enforce* certain rules of social conduct in a given geographical area," and sometimes as an institution that holds "a monopoly on the legal use of physical force" within such an area, is a "precondition of a civilized society."[16]

According to the Rand of the essay collections and the NBI lectures, every human being is, as Thomas Jefferson wrote in the Declaration of Independence, "endowed . . . with certain inalienable rights." Jefferson held that it was God, "[Man's] Creator," who had endowed people with these rights. Rand held that

[t]he source of man's rights is not divine law or congressional law, but the law of identity. A is A—and Man is Man. *Rights* are condi-

tions of existence required by man's nature for his proper survival. If man is to live on earth, it is *right* for him to use his mind, it is *right* to act on his own free judgment, it is *right* to work for his values and to keep the product of his work.[17]

"There is only *one* fundamental right," Rand contended: "a man's right to his own life." But to say that an individual has a right to his or her own life, she argued, is to say that that individual is entitled to "the freedom to take all the actions required by the nature of a rational being for the support, the furtherance, the fulfillment and the enjoyment of his own life."

And if "[t]he right to life is the source of all rights," Rand wrote, "the right to property is their only implementation. Without property rights, no other rights are possible. Since man has to sustain his life by his own effort, the man who has no right to the product of his effort has no means to sustain his life. The man who produces while others dispose of his product, is a slave."[18]

Since "[m]an's rights can be violated only by the use of physical force," Rand reasoned, "[t]he precondition of a civilized society is the barring of physical force from social relationships. . . . In a civilized society, force may be used only in retaliation and only against those who initiate its use."[19]

Yet "[i]f physical force is to be barred from social relationships," she wrote, "men need an institution charged with the task of protecting their rights under an *objective* code of rules.

"*This*," she concluded, "is the task of a government—of a *proper* government—its basic task, its only moral justification and the reason why men do need a government."[20]

In order to qualify as "proper," according to Rand, a government must be "rigidly defined, delimited and circumscribed"[21] as to its legitimate sphere(s) of action; it must not be "the *ruler,* but the servant or *agent* of the citizens."[22] It must confine itself to providing a police force "to protect men from criminals," a military force, "to protect men from foreign invaders," and a system of courts "to settle disputes among men according to objective laws."[23] In the Randian scheme of things, a proper government could have no power to tax, and would have to find voluntary means of raising the funds to finance its activities—by charging fees for its services, for example, and by holding lotteries.

"Anarchy, as a political concept," according to the Rand of the essay collections and the NBI lectures, "is a naive floating abstraction"; for "a society without an organized government would be at the mercy of the first criminal who came along and who would precipitate it into the chaos of gang warfare. But the possibility of human immorality is not the only objection to anarchy: even a society whose every member were fully rational and faultlessly moral, could not function in a state of anarchy; it is the need of *objectives* laws and of an arbiter for honest disagreements among men that necessitates the establishment of a government."[24]

Yet, in *Atlas Shrugged,* the utopian society established in "Galt's Gulch" by the novel's heroic characters, the striking "men of the mind"—"a society whose every member" *is* both "fully rational and faultlessly moral"—is an anarchist society. It is utterly without government of any kind. And it not only functions in this "state of anarchy," it functions very well indeed.

In effect, then, the millions of young people who read *Atlas Shrugged* during the 1960s learned from Ayn Rand that government was evil and unnecessary, while the tens of thousands of young people who joined the Objectivist movement during those same years learned from the very same teacher and theoretician that a carefully limited government is a necessary precondition of civilization. To her casual readers, Rand seemed an anarchist; to her most devoted students, she portrayed herself as an uncompromising minarchist. But always, to all comers, she was a libertarian.

Not that she ever acknowledged as much in so many words. From the beginning of her days as the leader of a movement,

Rand was absolutely consistent, not only in rejecting the libertarian label, but also in her insistence on portraying libertarianism as a sort of intellectual or philosophical heresy, a doctrine
fundamentally incompatible with Objectivism. During her years
as coleader of the Objectivist movement, she always tried to do
everything possible to prevent any association or contact of any
kind between Students of Objectivism and libertarians. To this
day, in fact, in the pages of the pathetic publications designed to
serve the pitiful remnant of the old Objectivist movement that is
now being run by Rand's longtime sycophant and toady Leonard
Peikoff, libertarianism is still routinely depicted as irreconcilable
with Objectivist doctrine; and association with libertarians and
their organizations by any Student of Objectivism is still considered grounds for what can only be described as excommunica-
tion from the Objectivist movement.

(In recent years, thanks mainly to the efforts of David Kelley,
a former philosophy professor at Vassar, the Objectivist movement has been surprisingly reinvigorated. Kelley, who has long
regarded libertarians as allies rather than enemies, was excommunicated from Peikoff's movement for daring to speak at an
event sponsored and attended by libertarians. Sensing that he
was not alone in feeling alienated by the parochial and exclu-
sionist behavior of the "official" Objectivist leaders, Kelley set
about raising money to create his own foundation, the Institute
for Objectivist Studies [IOS], and it is beneath the IOS umbrella
that Objectivism has, of late, begun to grow once more.)

For ten years, Rand and Branden pretty much succeeded in
their efforts to keep their Objectivist flock away from other libertarians; to an astonishing extent, they even managed to keep
their young Objectivist followers unaware of the very existence
of alternative kinds of libertarian thought and thinkers. Then, in
1968, in a fit of temper over a lover's quarrel with Branden that
had got seriously out of hand, Rand excommunicated her "intellectual heir" himself and forced him to close NBI. She continued

to edit and publish the *Objectivist* on her own for a few more months, then let it drop by the wayside as well. Rand utterly lacked Branden's executive ability, his ability to lead. It was he who had built her movement for her. And at that time, only he could keep that movement together, much less keep it growing.

8

The Modern Movement Comes Together

So, suddenly, in the late 1960s, in part because of some unintentionally good timing, because certain people were in the right place at the right time, because of what you might very well think of as an instance of what it means to describe something as being a result of human action but not of human design—namely, the fact that the major purges of libertarians from SDS and YAF and the collapse and disintegration of the Objectivist movement all happened at about the same time—a true, nationwide libertarian movement suddenly became possible. Suddenly, for the first time in many decades of American intellectual history, and *all at once, all at the same time,* a really substantial number of not left-wing or right-wing but *libertarian* political activists were all cut loose from their cultural moorings, from the institutional underpinnings in which they'd formed the habit of anchoring their libertarianism—all the clubs and societies and merchants and schools and think tanks and publications and activist groups and all the various ever-changing, ever-evolving interpersonal networks they'd grown used to having around and accessible and being able to depend upon during their years as libertarians. Not only were YAF, SDS, and NBI gone, along with their associated publications, institutions, and activities: LeFevre's Rampart College was gone too, along with *its* associated publications, institutions, and activities. Suddenly, just as popular demand for libertarian institutions strong enough to support an authentic, independent, frankly and explicitly libertarian political movement of truly nationwide scope seemed to reach a record high, institutions of exactly that kind began to disappear or become inaccessible to libertarians.

And, just as any free-market economist would have predicted, the invisible hand responded, creating a number of new institutions, the framework for a new libertarian movement.

In 1968, *Reason,* the first important libertarian journal of opinion, began regular monthly publication. Today, it is one of the top half-dozen opinion magazines in the country, with a paid circulation surpassed only by the *National Review,* the *New Republic,* the *Nation, Commentary,* and the *American Spectator.* And its parent corporation, the Reason Foundation, is now the second largest and second most influential of a whole batch of new libertarian public-policy research institutions, or "think tanks," none of which existed at all about twenty years ago.

The largest and most influential of these organizations, the Washington, D.C.–based Cato Institute, was established in 1977. Like the Reason Foundation, Cato is a large-scale operation that spends several million dollars every year on an ambitious program of publications and conferences. By doing so, it has, like Reason, established its credibility with government officials, other policy makers, and members of the media, thereby guaranteeing a serious hearing for its research and its proposals among those whose judgments determine the sort of future we can all expect to face in the decades to come.

Cato and Reason are the most conspicuous of the libertarian

"think tanks" that have sprung up in the past two decades, but they are by no means the only ones. Several smaller institutions are now engaged in similar work on a more modest scale. Some of them, like the Institute for Humane Studies, which was already active during the 1960s, have been given a new lease on life and new access to larger resources by the libertarian boom of the '70s and '80s, and '90s. Others, like the Mises Institute, the Center for the Study of Market Processes, the Agorist Institute, the Center for Independent Thought, and the Competitive Enterprise Institute, have been newly launched since 1970.

The past two decades have also seen a significant increase in the libertarian presence in the major media. Twenty years ago, it was unusual, to say the very least, to see an editorial or opinion column expressing the libertarian point of view in one of the nation's top newspapers. Twenty years ago, the libertarian point of view was generally regarded as part of the "lunatic fringe" and therefore unworthy of publication. Today, there are several nationally syndicated political columnists—Stephen Chapman, Doug Bandow, and Vin Suprynowicz among them—who espouse the libertarian point of view. And such libertarian writers as David Boaz, Patrick Cox, Tom Hazlett, Robert Poole, Lynn Scarlett, Ted Galen Carpenter, Ed Crane, and the late John Dentinger have provided reams of copy for the opinion pages of papers like the *Wall Street Journal, USA Today,* the *New York Times,* the *Los Angeles Times,* and the *Chicago Tribune* over the past fifteen years. Meanwhile, the *Orange County Register,* the flagship publication of the Freedom Newspapers chain founded during the 1930s by R. C. Hoiles, has become the third largest daily paper in California (surpassed only by the *Los Angeles Times* and the *San Francisco Chronicle*), the twenty-fourth largest daily in the nation, and the second most profitable daily in the nation (surpassed as a moneymaker only by the *Los Angeles Times*). The *Register*—which is to the Los Angeles metropolitan area more or less what *Newsday* is to the New York metropolitan area—is no longer run by R. C. Hoiles himself. "The old man," as he is still referred to by more than a few old hands at the paper, died in 1981, at the age of ninety-two. But the *Register,* and all the other thirty or so Freedom Newspapers, are still fairly consistent exponents of the Hoiles philosophy on their editorial pages. The *Register*'s daily editorials still call for abolition of the public schools and abolition of taxes, just as they did in R. C. Hoiles's day. They still call for free trade, free immigration, and a firm policy of keeping the U.S. government's nose (and money and manpower and weaponry) out of other sovereign nations' business—both their internal affairs and their relations with one another. The *Register* still publishes excerpts from the writings of R. C. Hoiles himself in its weekly (Sunday) Commentary section. And, with respect both to circulation and to revenues, the *Register* is one of the most rapidly growing daily newspapers in the United States.

For ten years, the Libertarian Party (LP), which had been founded in a Denver, Colorado, living room in 1971 by a few dozen former YAFers, SDSers, and Students of Objectivism, established an impressive record of fast and steady growth. The party's first presidential candidate, philosophy professor John Hospers, appeared on the ballot in only a handful of states when he ran in 1972 and attracted only around five thousand popular votes nationwide—plus one electoral vote cast by a renegade Republican elector from Virginia named Roger MacBride. In 1976, when MacBride himself ran for president on the LP ticket, he managed to qualify his candidacy for ballot status in most states and collected around a quarter of a million votes. In 1980, the third LP presidential candidate, Ed Clark, not only became the first third-party presidential nominee in decades to get his name on the ballot in all fifty states, he also persuaded a cool million American voters to cast their ballots for him. And by that time the LP had actually elected a handful of state and local officials here and there around the country. So, all in all, the party's future looked rosy.

But as things turned out, the LP had peaked—reached its apparent limits—in 1980. Its presidential campaigns since then have been progressively less successful. The party had a certain appeal at first, especially among younger voters who had discovered during their years of protesting the Vietnam war and the draft that neither the Democratic Party of Lyndon Johnson and Hubert Humphrey nor the Republican Party of Richard Nixon had anything whatever to offer them. The LP introduced the libertarian idea—the "freedom philosophy," as Robert LeFevre always preferred to call it—to hundreds of thousands of people who had never heard of it before. Still, as things turned out, the party's appeal simply wasn't as strong as the appeal of boycotting elections altogether.

9

The Nonvoters

Deliberate nonvoting has a long history as a libertarian strategy, especially among anarchists. As one European anarchist wrote in 1904:

> The voter is a man who comes where he is summoned one day like
> a flunkey, to one who whistles for him as for a dog trained to obey,
> who comes on the said day only and not on any other day. He is a
> man who comes when authority says: "The moment is here to sanc-
> tion one more time a system established by others and for others than
> yourself. The moment is here to choose those who will be part of this
> system . . . those who, for contributing to the functioning of the
> machine that crushes the weak, will be paid in silver, in influence, in
> privileges, in honors. The moment is here to put aside one more time
> the idea of revolt against the organization that exploits you and to
> obey its authority. The moment is here to vote, that is to say, to make
> an act which signifies: I RECOGNIZE YOUR LAWS."
>
> Is it not clear that the first meaning of abstaining from elections
> is this: "I DO NOT RECOGNIZE THE LAWS"?[25]

American anarchists of this same period like Benjamin R.
Tucker argued, as American anarchists of the previous century

73

had argued before them, that any true advocate of individual liberty must refuse to participate in elections, because voting is tantamount to acknowledging the legitimacy of the political process, the system government uses to sustain and expand its power over the individual. Sixty years later, all over the country, especially on places like campuses where there were large concentrations of young people, this argument suddenly began popping up again. In Southern California in the late 1960s, for example, a libertarian named Sy Leon started the League of Non-Voters. Leon had worked closely for many years with Robert LeFevre, as a teacher and administrator at both the Freedom School and Rampart College; he had also put in some time as a regional business representative for the Nathaniel Branden Institute. He financed his campaign against voting mainly by selling pins and bumperstickers that read: "Don't Vote—It Only Encourages Them."

Later Leon modified his position somewhat, arguing in a book entitled *None of the Above* that citizens should refuse to vote at least until all ballots were changed to include the choice "None of the Above." Leon also proposed that any office won by "None of the Above" in an election remain unfilled until such time as a new election could be held with entirely different candidates; the old candidates, the candidates in the original election, the candidates who had already lost once to "None of the Above," would be banned from any and all future races for that office.

It has long been fashionable among political reporters to attribute both low voter turnouts in particular elections and years of steady decline in voter turnout for elections in general to "apathy." But virtually all the available evidence suggests that this explanation is completely bogus.

As early as 1975, in a study entitled *Political Alienation in Contemporary America,* two University of Michigan political scientists, Robert S. Gilmour and Robert B. Lamb, after carefully considering all the various factors that might have contributed to the steady decline in voter participation in national elections since midcentury, concluded that the chief cause of the decline was the widespread belief that voting was futile because there were almost never any significant differences among the candidates competing for any particular office.

This is *not* "apathy." Apathy is indifference, lack of interest. If I say that voting in a particular election is futile, I am *not* saying that I am indifferent to or uninterested in the outcome of that election; I am saying that, however interesting I may consider the election, I believe that casting a vote in it cannot make any significant difference in its outcome.

In his book *Great Expectations: America and the Baby Boom Generation,* Landon Y. Jones noted that, as of 1980, the members of the '60s generation had "not followed the traditional pattern of embracing political parties as they grow older. Unlike their parents, this generation has remained independent."

As Jones saw it, "the baby boom was young during . . . Vietnam and Watergate and learned then its continuing distrust of the political system." The attitude that was "typical of baby boom politics," in 1980 he said flat out, was "anti-government." And, he argued, "the fact that the political parties cannot effectively organize the opinion of the baby boom has contributed to the decline of the parties themselves and, indirectly, to the decline of voter participation."[26]

Another book of the same year which was credited in its time with doing a particularly exemplary job of identifying the fundamental, underlying values and attitudes of the baby boom generation, Marilyn Ferguson's *The Aquarian Conspiracy,* lamented that "we have relinquished more and more autonomy to the state, forcing government to assume functions once performed by communities, families, churches—*people.* Many social tasks have reverted to government by default, and the end result has been creeping paralysis. . . ."[27]

Ferguson quoted Tocqueville's 150-year-old warning against

the sort of government that "covers the surface of society with a network of small, complicated rules, minute and uniform, through which the most original minds and the most energetic characters cannot penetrate"; the sort of government that serves as "the sole agent of happiness" for its citizens; which "provides for their security, foresees and supplies their necessities, facilitates their pleasures, manages their principal concerns, directs their industry, regulates the descent of property, and subdivides their inheritances—what remains," Tocqueville demanded, "but to spare them all the care of thinking and the trouble of living?"

"Such a power," Tocqueville warned, "does not tyrannize but it compresses, enervates, extinguishes and stupefies a people. The nation is nothing better than a flock of timid and industrious animals of which the government is the shepherd."

Ferguson saw a trend in the politics of the baby boom generation which she believed was leading our society in an entirely different direction from this, in the direction of a kind of individualism which she called *autarchy*. This is, of course, the very same term which the pacifist-anarchist-libertarian Robert LeFevre began using in the mid-1960s to describe his own doctrine. And Ferguson defined it exactly as LeFevre did. "*Autarchy*," LeFevre wrote, "is *self-rule*. It means that each person rules himself, and no other."[28] "*Autarchy*," says Ferguson, "is government by the self."[29]

LeFevre used to say that the only way to create a truly free society was one individual at a time: some individual would begin the process by resolving to rule himself, and no other; then another individual would make the same decision for herself; then another; then another; and so on. Similarly, Ferguson wrote that "the new political awareness has little to do with parties or ideologies. Its constituents don't come in blocs. Power that is never surrendered by the individual cannot be brokered."

The new political awareness, Ferguson wrote, will not come "by revolution or protest but by autonomy"; it is in this way and only in this way, she insisted, that the day will dawn when "the old slogan becomes a surprising fact: *Power to the people.* One by one by one."[30]

In yet another 1980 book on the emerging politics of the baby boom generation, Kirkpatrick Sale's *Human Scale,* we were informed that "many years ago—nearly a hundred, in fact—a publication called *The Rebel,* put out in Boston, carried this editorial from one Arthur Arnould:

> An individual eats some mushrooms and is poisoned by them. The doctor gives him an emetic and cures him. He goes to the cook and says to him:
>
> —"The mushrooms in white sauce made me ill yesterday! Tomorrow you must prepare them with brown sauce."
>
> Our individual eats the mushrooms in brown sauce. Second poisoning, second visit of the doctor, and second cure by the emetic.
>
> —"By Jove!" says he to the cook. "I want no more mushrooms with brown or white sauce, to-morrow you must fry them."
>
> Third poisoning, with accompaniment of doctor and emetic.
>
> —"This time," cries our friend, "they shall not catch me again! . . . to-morrow you must preserve them in sugar."
>
> The preserved mushrooms poison him again.
>
> —"But that man is an imbecile!" you say. "Why does he not throw away his mushrooms and stop eating them."
>
> Be less severe, I beg you, because that imbecile is yourself, it is ourselves, it is all humanity.
>
> Here are four to five thousand years that you try the State—that is to say Power, Authority, Government—in all kinds of sauces, that you make, unmake, cut, and pare down constitutions of all patterns, and still the poisoning goes on. You have tried legitimate royalty, manufactured royalty, parliamentary royalty, republics unitary and centralized, and the only thing from which you suffer, the despotism, the dictature of the State, you have scrupulously respected and carefully preserved.

"I do not claim," Sale comments, "that Americans in any great numbers are yet prepared to do away with the state that has made them so ill. But I do not believe I am wrong in detecting the beginnings, the stirrings, the growth, of a true antimushroom sentiment in the land: people who, perhaps only dimly, have come to realize—in a way that even Common Cause does not yet understand—that 'the government cannot solve the problem because the government is the problem.' Inchoate, to be sure, unexpressed except by a few, this sentiment is nonetheless found today in a thousand guises."[31]

10

Neither Left Nor Right

"It has become a cliche," wrote David Boaz in his introduction to a 1986 Cato Institute book entitled *Left, Right and Baby Boom,*

> to say that the baby boomers are fiscally conservative [that is, opposed to government interference with what Harvard philosopher Robert Nozick calls "capitalist acts between consenting adults"] and socially liberal [that is, opposed to government interference in the personal lives and habits of individuals], but cliches are often founded on truth. Polls do show this generation to be more conservative on economic issues than older voters, while they retain the social liberalism—or tolerance, as ['80s Republican campaign consultant] Lee Atwater more accurately calls it—acquired during the Sixties.[32]

Late in 1985, *Fortune* magazine reported that a survey of "baby-boom business leaders" showed most of them to be "neither consistent liberals nor conservatives," but rather libertarians, who "oppose government intervention in both the economy and their personal lives." Another study conducted in the mid-1980s by D. Quinn Mills of the Harvard Business School found that 60 percent of baby-boom-generation business executives could be considered politically libertarian.

Within a decade after the official close of the '60s, there were at least two runaway libertarian bestsellers—Harry Browne's *How I Found Freedom in an Unfree World* (a ringing call for a self-interested abandonment of politics) and Robert J. Ringer's *Restoring the American Dream*—as well as at least one major libertarian *succes d'estime,* Robert Nozick's National Book Award–winning *Anarchy, State and Utopia.*

All this would make perfect sense if we had begun with the assumption that the main political thrust of the youth rebellion of the '60s was libertarian. But if, instead, we begin with the conventional assumption that the youth rebellion of that period was politically on the Left, how are we to account for all this? How do we even *begin* to *try* to account for it? If the baby boom generation had been mainly left of center in its politics, you'd expect the 1970s and 1980s to have witnessed dramatic growth in leftist think tanks, not libertarian think tanks. You'd expect that the most successful new opinion magazine of the '70s and '80s would have been a leftist publication, not a libertarian publication. You'd expect to have seen a major increase in the numbers of articles and writers pushing a left-wing point of view on the opinion pages of our nation's newspapers over the past two decades, not a major increase in the numbers of articles and writers pushing a libertarian point of view. You'd expect that it would have been leftists, not libertarians, who would have enjoyed the most success trying to launch and build a new political party during the '70s and '80s. (Yet, when Barry Commoner ran for president in 1980 as the candidate of the left-wing Citizens' Party, he was able to muster only about one-fourth as many votes as that year's Libertarian Party candidate.)

The conventional explanation of all these anomalies is that

the baby boomers have changed their political views over the years. They were leftists during the '60s, it is said, but they have abandoned their old ideals and principles since then. And, of course, it is easy enough to find specific cases in which this seems to be exactly what has occurred. Peter Collier and David Horowitz, for example, who certainly *seemed* to be leftists when they were editing *Ramparts* magazine back in the late 1960s, have since published books renouncing their earlier left-wing views and announcing their conversion to what I suppose could best be described as a variety of Reagan Republicanism.

But is it really plausible to hypothesize that an entire generation has changed its mind in this way? It seems to me that we have an alternative hypothesis available to us, and that this alternative hypothesis is both much more plausible and much easier to reconcile with the public behavior of the baby boom generation in the years since the tempestuous 1960s came to an end.

Briefly, that alternative hypothesis is as follows: the overwhelming majority of the millions of young people who protested the Vietnam War and the draft during the 1960s were never leftists in the first place.

Certainly, the majority of the speakers at the antiwar and antidraft rallies and demonstrations of the period were leftists—New Leftists, to be exact. It was the New Left that organized most of the rallies and demonstrations, and it is hardly surprising that, being in control of the show, they put their own people up in front of it, right smack in center stage.

And, of course, once those New Leftists were on stage, they presented *their* reasons for opposing the war and the draft. To oversimplify somewhat (but not, I think, overmuch), they explained that the U.S. government was propping up the South Vietnamese government and helping it fight a war against the Vietnamese communists because the U.S. government was an imperialist power, bent on building a worldwide empire of Third World countries run by puppet governments—an empire not unlike the one built and maintained earlier by England. Since all people everywhere have an inalienable right to political self-determination, the New Leftists argued, the United States should withdraw from Vietnam and allow the people of that country to make their own decisions about what kind of government they wanted. Moreover, the New Leftists said, it was only the existence of the draft which made the imperialist foreign policies of the U.S. government possible, by guaranteeing it a virtually unending supply of manpower to devote to its imperialist military activities; therefore, the draft should be abolished.

Now, consider two points.

First, the reasons for opposing the Vietnam War and the draft which I have just sketched—the reasons expounded upon incessantly during the '60s by the New Left—are not the only possible reasons one might have for taking these positions, that is, opposing the war and the draft.

Second, from the fact that a great many people cheer wildly when a speaker at a rally demands U.S. withdrawal from Vietnam and abolition of compulsory military service, it does *not* follow that all those cheering people support the speaker's policy proposals *for the same reasons*.

Suppose for a moment that you were a nineteen-year-old college student back in 1968 and that you had been converted to pacifism. Your opposition to all violence would lead you inexorably to oppose all war. It might easily lead you to oppose compulsory military service as well, on the grounds that since the ultimate purpose or raison d'etre of any armed force is to use violence against other human beings, it is impossible to work in any capacity for a military organization, even as a typist or cook, without lending aid and support to the cause of violence.

Or suppose you were a young libertarian who believed that just as *taxation* is merely a fancy word meant to justify what is more accurately described as robbery, so *war* is merely a fancy word meant to justify mass murder, and *military conscription* is merely a fancy phrase meant to justify what the U.S. Constitution calls "involuntary servitude," that is, slavery.

Or suppose you were simply a young person who wasn't much interested in politics at all—the sort of person who would never even consider joining a political activist group or reading books about political philosophy or subscribing to a political magazine; the sort of person who really just wants to live your own life and cultivate your own garden without having to worry about being hassled and interfered with by other people, particularly other people who are perfect strangers to you, people of whom you can quite truthfully say that you never did anything to *them,* never tried to interfere in *their* lives, never gave *them* any reason to make trouble for *you.*

All three of these hypothetical young people would have been likely to turn out for a demonstration against the war and the draft during the '60s—the first two because they held certain political views (but *not,* notice, the political views of the New Left), the third for purely personal reasons like fear of violent death and a general distaste for the idea of traveling halfway around the world in order to shoot at people you don't know and with whom you have had no quarrel.

I have pointed out that the antiwar and antidraft rallies and demonstrations of the '60s were organized by the New Left, and, therefore, addressed almost exclusively by New Left speakers. Under the circumstances, this was inevitable. Rallies and demonstrations are not organized by nonpolitical people like the third of the three hypothetical young people whose reasons for being against the war and the draft I just described. Rallies and demonstrations are organized by political activists. In the '60s, young political activists came in three types, as we have seen: the right-wingers, the leftists, and the libertarians. The right-wingers certainly weren't going to organize antiwar and antidraft rallies: at the time the student movement against the war and the draft first got underway, the Right supported both U.S. military involvement in Southeast Asia and the policy of conscription. The libertarians were unlikely to organize the antiwar and antidraft rallies and demonstrations, for, as has been noted, when those rallies and demonstrations first began happening, the libertarians on campus were not yet numerous enough or organized enough to assume a leading role of that kind.

By default, therefore, the New Left found itself confronted with an opportunity to, in effect, get out in front of a parade that was already on the move, an opportunity to coopt a spontaneous, grassroots protest movement without even having to best any rivals in the process. It was convenient, to be sure, that the New Leftists—some of them, at any rate—actually knew a thing or two about how to go about organizing rallies and demonstrations. Some of the older SDSers had been systematically trained in certain of the relevant skills by the same professional labor organizers on whom they relied for most of their funding; others of them had picked up hands-on experience as activists in the civil rights movement of the early '60s. It was much easier back then to find an experienced political organizer among the New Leftists than among either the right-wingers or the libertarians. In that sense, the New Left was better qualified to take over the "leadership" of the antiwar and antidraft movement.

But mainly what the New Leftists had was the opportunity—the opportunity and the common, ordinary horse sense to recognize a once-in-a-lifetime opportunity when they saw one. They knew that if they organized the rallies and the demonstrations and the marches and then got out in front of all the protesters and hogged the show and presented themselves to the media as the legitimate spokesmen for all those protesters, the media would very likely buy their scam and give them credit on national TV and in public print for having a lot more followers than they really had. And they did it, and it worked. They bamboozled the media, and the media bamboozled the public. And to this day, most Americans still believe that most of the youthful protesters of the 1960s were leftists.

Yet consider: as soon as the draft was abolished and the U.S. government began withdrawing from the Vietnam War, the overwhelming majority of the young protesters vanished overnight. If they had been leftists, would they have done so? If they had been leftists, wouldn't they have turned their attention to other leftist causes, like economic democracy, and gone right on rallying and protesting, following the lead of their self-proclaimed "leaders"?

Interestingly, the "Woodstock Census" makes obvious how little influence the leaders of the New Left actually exercised over their supposed followers. When Weiner and Stillman asked their respondents to name the individuals who had most influenced them and excited their admiration during the '60s, not a single one of the New Left activists identified by the mass media at the time as "leaders" of the antiwar/antidraft movement even made it into the top ten. Tom Hayden, who finished the best of the lot, seems to have influenced and won the admiration of scarcely a quarter of those responding.

No. The mainstream of the antiwar/antidraft movement of the 1960s was never on the Left. From the beginning, it was, broadly speaking, libertarian. That is, your typical movement person was usually very suspicious of government in general, government as such, and he or she also usually favored less of any kind of government interference with individuals, whether the meddling was directed at the economic side—the time we spend as buyers, sellers, investors, employers, employees, and managers in the marketplace, the world of business and money— or at the personal side of our lives. In this same broad sense, the politics of the baby boom generation as a whole is libertarian, and always has been. This is why the years since the '60s have seen the steady decline of the Left juxtaposed with the steady growth of libertarianism.

Not that the libertarian quadrant of the American political spectrum was the only one that grew during the '70s and '80s. The conservative or right-wing quadrant also grew rapidly throughout this period. Indeed, in some respects, the achievements of the conservatives over the past three decades have far surpassed any comparable gains by the libertarians. The biggest of the newer conservative think tanks, the Heritage Foundation, operates on a level that dwarfs the efforts of all the new libertarian think tanks combined. Where the libertarians have won a few small offices and attracted a million votes for one of their presidential candidates, the conservatives have put their man in the White House twice in a row.

Not only that, they seem to have put him there partly with the help of baby-boom-generation voters. By a wide margin, those baby boomers who voted at all in the 1980 and 1984 presidential elections, for example, voted for Ronald Reagan, not for his libertarian or left-wing opponents. Clearly, then, there is nothing monolithically libertarian about the politics of the baby boom generation as a whole.

This point is borne out further by the fact that one of the most successful of the new conservative opinion journalists who first began rising to prominence during the 1970s and 1980s is a baby boomer named R. Emmett Tyrrell Jr. As a student and card-carrying YAF member at Indiana University during the '60s, Tyrrell founded a monthly journal of conservative opinion which he called the *Alternative*. After graduating, he kept his magazine going, moving it first to a small office near the Indiana University campus in Bloomington; then, some years later, after rechristening it the *American Spectator,* to Washington, D.C.

Reason, which I described earlier as the most successful of the libertarian political magazines to emerge during the '70s and '80s, was launched at about the same time as Tyrrell's *American Spectator.* But of the two, it is the *American Spectator* that has enjoyed the greater success. And the *Spectator*'s success has greatly benefited its founder and editor, enabling him to find major publishers for several collections of the essays and editorials he has written for his magazine over the years, enabling him to find a publisher (if only a fairly rabid right-wing publisher) for his heavily opinionated and satirical "biography" of Bill Clinton, and—perhaps most important—making it possible for him to set up shop as a nationally syndicated political columnist.

In fact, despite the considerable success his magazine has enjoyed in recent years, Tyrrell himself is best known today not as an editor but as a writer. And thereby hangs a tale, for Tyrrell as a writer is a very curious case indeed. Whatever he may have accomplished as an editor, he has accomplished something as a writer that would seem at first glance to be virtually impossible: he has founded an entire career on nothing more than the extraordinarily careful imitation of an earlier man of letters with whom, really, he has almost nothing at all in common.

11

Who Is R. Emmett Tyrrell Jr.? or The Ersatz Mencken of the American Right

Indeed, if imitation is the sincerest form of flattery, then R. Emmett Tyrrell Jr. has flattered H. L. Mencken more sincerely by far than any of the Sage of Baltimore's many other idolatrous fans has ever done—more sincerely, one might even venture to say, than anyone has ever before flattered a man of letters of Mencken's eminence. Flattery *this* sincere is more commonly associated with the world of popular entertainment (and especially with the world of commercial broadcast television, where it has long since been elevated to the status of a governing principle) than with the world of serious literature. Perhaps this is why it is the world of popular entertainment that seems readiest to hand with fully comparable cases.

One can search through all of American literature and not find Tyrrell's like anywhere. But in the world of popular entertainment, Tyrrell's like is legion. One might easily say, for example, that Tyrrell is to H. L. Mencken as the Beach Boys were to the Four Freshmen, or as Brenda Lee was to Kay Starr, or as Brook Benton was to Nat "King" Cole. For what these various pop singers imitated was not the particular songs of their models, but their overall "sound"—the *style* in which their models presented their songs. And what Tyrrell has chosen to imitate in Mencken is not the particular ideas he expressed, but his *style,* his overall way of writing.

And his imitation is thoroughgoing, there's no getting around that. Tyrrell has obviously done his homework. He's picked up on Mencken's characteristic way with adjectives, his hyperbole, his sonorous cadences, his technique of salting a more or less traditionally literary and essayistic manner with outbursts of slang, even his clownish titles—witness "Richard Milhous Nixon and the Serenade in B-Flat" and "Betty Friedan and the Women of the Fevered Brow" from Tyrrell's very first collection of his *Alternative* and *American Spectator* pieces, *Public Nuisances* (1979).

But look past the surface, the packaging; look past the manner of presentation and fix your attention on the matter being presented, and you will come face to face with the profound difference between H. L. Mencken and R. Emmett Tyrrell Jr.

Where Mencken stood steadfast against all war, even opposing U.S. involvement in both World War I and World War II, Tyrrell is a militarist warmonger of the very worst sort, bent on whitewashing and "rehabilitating" the U.S. government's sorry record of military involvement in Southeast Asia during the 1960s and on justifying the "necessity" of U.S. military involvement in Africa and the Middle East during the '70s to "defend" those parts of the world against the "Soviet menace." During the '80s and '90s he has gone on to provide Menckenesque "justifications" for the absurd Reagan and Bush adventures in Grenada, Panama, and the Middle East.

Where Mencken believed in what he called "free competition in all human enterprises, and to the utmost limit," Tyrrell comes out firmly against what he terms "absolute license," whether in regard to regulation of commerce, the tax code, or whatever.

Where Mencken advocated untrammeled freedom of expression (he once deliberately got himself arrested on the Boston Common by selling a policeman an issue of his magazine, the *American Mercury,* which had been legally banned in that city), Tyrrell argues that "intelligent people can distinguish pornography from art," and that "the rights of the pornographer can be balanced against the rights of a community that judges pornography baneful."

According to Tyrrell, "one can make pornography less accessible without banning it totally," and therefore "the claim that by regulating pornography's availability America glissades down a slippery slope toward total censorship is pristine and exquisite balderdash."

Mencken himself couldn't have put it any differently or any better—except, of course, that Mencken himself would never have said it at all.

There is irony in the fact that H. L. Mencken, of all writers, should have been imitated in such a thoughtless and superficial way as this. For it was Mencken who wrote, back in 1926, that

> the essence of a sound style is . . . that it is a living and breathing thing . . . that it fits its proprietor tightly and yet ever so loosely, as his skin fits him. It is, in fact, quite as securely an integral part of him as that skin is. It hardens as his arteries harden. It . . . is always the outward and visible symbol of a man, and it cannot be anything else.[33]

Yet here is R. Emmett Tyrrell Jr. borrowing another man's skin, borrowing the outward and visible symbol of a man utterly unlike himself and trying to live within it. Reading him is rather like going to a dinner party and meeting this unbelievably obnoxious character who, you're assured beforehand, does this absolutely *fabulous* W. C. Fields impression. As it turns out, he does. Oh, it's not really absolutely fabulous, but it's not bad. It is, however, rather hollow, because all the impressionist has mastered is the externals, the surface, the mannerisms. And his impression therefore lacks content.

But he performs quite willingly, for all that. In fact, he goes on and on and on all evening long, doing his impression of W. C. Fields. No matter what topic you steer the conversation toward, no matter what sorts of things you try to get him talking about, even when you ask him if he'd like more coffee or which way it is to the restroom, he does it all in his W. C. Fields voice, complete with all the mannerisms. It wears on you after a while. And when the evening is over and you can go home—or close the book—it is a genuine relief.

12

The <u>Other</u> Youth Rebellion of the 1960s

Tyrrell's success underscores the very same lesson that Ronald Reagan's proven ability to win votes from baby boomers proves beyond question: not all baby boomers are libertarians. The baby boom generation has a strong, deeply conservative streak running through it as well. Millions of other baby boomers are liberals or populists.

But the number of Americans who can be classified either as liberals or as populists has been declining steadily for a quarter-century or more, while the number who can be classified as conservatives or libertarians has been just as steadily growing. And, since young conservatives have been markedly more successful than young libertarians in recent decades at the job of consolidating and institutionalizing their newfound influence and using it to attain and exercise real political power, shouldn't I perhaps consider arguing that the political essence, the political heart of the baby boom generation, the political orientation that typifies and is most accurately representative of

93

the basic spirit of that generation is not libertarianism, but con-
servatism?

I have considered this question at great length, and I have
determined that no, the baby boom generation is not conservative,
not *really,* not in its heart of hearts. If it were, why would the most
successful conservative writer to emerge from the baby boom
generation thus far find it necessary to imitate a libertarian writer
of an earlier time in order to achieve that success? If the baby
boom generation were conservative in its heart of hearts, would it
have turned out in such phenomenal, unheard of numbers thirty-
five years ago to protest the draft and the Vietnam War?

Which is more important? The fact that most baby boomers
who vote at all support conservative candidates? Or the fact that
most baby boomers don't vote at all? For "is it not clear that the
first meaning of abstaining from elections is this: 'I DO NOT
RECOGNIZE THE LAWS'?"

On the other hand, the mass media did the American people
another disservice back in the 1960s by glossing over or ignoring
entirely in their coverage of the youth rebellion of that period the
important distinction between the young rebels who told us to
oppose the war and the draft and demanded political reform and the
young rebels who told us, "Do your own thing!" and demanded
cultural change—the crucially important distinction between the
ideologues and foot-soldier activists of "The Movement" and the
"hippies" and "flower children" of the "Counterculture."

These latter, the cultural rebels of the time, were always
much more numerous than their political counterparts; and their
role in shaping the most profound of the many changes we've
seen sweeping through American society during the last twenty-
five years—I refer to the genuinely revolutionary changes that
have transformed the very fabric of our national way of life—has
been immeasurably greater.

"But what," I hear someone asking, "does it mean to say that
someone is a *cultural* rebel? What is a 'culture,' anyway?"

A culture is a spontaneously ordered system—a system which is "the result of human action but not of human design," a system which was never planned by anyone or any conspiracy, a system which simply "arose" or "came into being" as the unforeseen and unintended consequence of billions and billions of actions undertaken separately by millions upon millions of different individuals who have not been in collusion or even "in touch" with each other in any other way. Like all spontaneously ordered systems, a culture changes constantly, remakes itself constantly. Yet, viewed over time (and again, like all other systems of its type), every culture also exhibits a kind of stability, some quality or group of qualities that seems somehow to persist through change, so that it makes sense to speak of a particular culture as having a certain basic underlying character, a certain essence, a certain *identity,* and to speak of cultures as being different from or similar to each other.

Viewed over time by an outside observer, the social behavior of any people will appear to be consistently in accord with certain rules. Viewed over time by an outside observer, the behavior of any people in any society will be seen to be exactly what it would have been if it had been deliberately calculated in order to conform to certain principles or to carry out some preconceived plan. Viewed over time by an outside observer, human social behavior is inevitably seen to display order, not disorder.

But there are two types of order—imposed order and spontaneous order. And very little of the order we discover in human social behavior if we observe it over time has been imposed from without. Laws are imposed on us, of course; to the extent that people behave as they do because the law requires it, to that extent we can say that the order we observe in society is imposed on it by design, according to some plan.

But what extent are we talking about here? On examination, I submit that it turns out not to amount to much at all. Only a small fraction of most people's daily activities are prescribed by law. The law doesn't tell us how to dress, for example, or which utensils to use when we dine, or how often we should dine, or what we should and should not eat, or what religious beliefs to hold, or what entertainment to enjoy, or how to conduct our love lives, or where to live, or what kind of work to do, or how to furnish and decorate our homes.

Still, we act as though we are following rules in all these aspects of our lives, just as we do in those situations in which our behavior really *is* determined by rules. We dress one way if we're women, another way if we're men; we dress one way to attend a business meeting, another way to attend a baseball game; we take it for granted that the man will assume all the responsibility for initiating any social or sexual contact he may ever have with any woman, and that when a woman marries, she will adopt her husband's surname as her own; we take it for granted also that while it is only natural and proper to slaughter cattle and pigs for their meat, it is disgusting and perverse even to *talk* about slaughtering horses, dogs, and cats for the same reason.

There are no laws requiring that we behave in any of these ways. Yet we do, and so predictably, so consistently, that, viewed over time and from outside, our behavior looks just as rulebound as it would if there were such laws in effect.

In one sense, our behavior *is* rulebound, but not by rules anyone has imposed upon us, rather by rules which have emerged spontaneously from the process of social interaction itself.

The sum of all the rules of social interaction that emerge spontaneously in any particular society is the *culture* that holds that society together. Culture is the basic glue that holds any human society together. Culture is the most fundamental of the various spontaneously ordered systems—language, the market— which we find in all human societies.

It is easy enough to see why most of us obey the law most of the time: we submit to the order imposed upon us by government because we have been threatened with imprisonment and seizure of our property if we do otherwise. It is perhaps less evident that we follow the rules that make up the culture we live in for much the same reason—that we fear the consequences of not doing so. True, no one threatens us with imprisonment or expropriation if we defy the rules of our culture. But we all grow up knowing, nevertheless, that he (or she) who defies the culture risks another sort of punishment—the punishment we call *ostracism.*

Our culture regards certain ways of schooling the young, certain ways of healing the sick, certain ways of theorizing about scientific matters, and certain ways of practicing religious beliefs as legitimate and respectable; others it regards as illegitimate and unworthy of respect. Our culture considers certain styles—in the arts, in clothing, in family life and elsewhere—to be acceptable; others it considers unacceptable.

Over time, powerful institutions have come into being to promote the ways and styles of living which our culture endorses—churches; schools; medical, scientific, and educational associations. These institutions are "private" in the sense that they have no power to stamp out alternative ways and styles by law. But they exercise a very real power, nevertheless.

Anyone who seeks a career in education, in healing, in the sciences, or in the arts knows that any failure to toe the cultural line, any failure to go along with tradition, can lead to disaster. Defy the culture, and you risk not being taken seriously. Defy the culture, and you risk being passed over for good jobs, for promotions, for the chance to advance to positions of influence in your field. Follow the rules; respect the authority of tradition. This is the road to success.

In American society in 1964, the prevailing expectation was that every individual would dress and groom himself according to whatever happened to be the style of the moment within his particular cultural niche. The expectation was that businessmen would dress as businessmen were "supposed" to dress, that students would dress as students were "supposed" to dress, and so forth.

In America in 1964, any writer who dared to question the pronouncements of the "experts" so denominated by the organizations and institutions traditionally accorded the most respect within those experts' fields—anyone who dared to question the medical profession's views on health and healing, or the educational establishment's views on schooling, or organized Christianity's views on spiritual matters—found himself unable to find a publisher.

Creative individuals in the America of 1964—whether they were painters, composers, artists, or what have you—were expected to create within the boundaries and limitations of traditional styles and genres and to refrain from eclectic borrowing and combining of techniques and ideas that most other people in the past had regarded as belonging to different and irreconcilable categories.

The hippies of the counterculture rebelled against this way of looking at things. The men grew beards, grew their hair to shoulder length and beyond, and wore that hair in ponytails. The women wore dresses that hadn't been in style since their grandmothers' day.

The hippies experimented openly with nutritional theories and with systems of healing like chiropractic, naturopathy, and acupuncture which, in the view of the mainstream of American society, had long since been discredited by the duly constituted and established authorities. They began experimenting spiritually too—fooling around with unfamiliar religions from remote and exotic parts of the world like Hinduism and Buddhism, and also with the long since discredited notions of occultists, astrologers, readers of auras, numerologists, and devotees of Tarot cards and the I Ching.

They decorated their homes in wildly eclectic fashion, borrowing something here and something else there, so that Aubrey

Beardsley, Maxfield Parrish, M. C. Escher, Rene Magritte, Hieronymous Bosch, and Ansel Adams shared the same room with madras curtains and tablecloths and Tiffany-style lamps. They adopted rock 'n' roll as their favorite kind of music—rock, a hybrid genre which had been created by freely mixing elements borrowed from black blues with still other elements borrowed from country music. Rock—a music eclectic down to its very roots, down to the depths of its soul; a music born in eclectic disregard of traditional categories and the expectations of other people; a music that depended for its ongoing enrichment and development on musicians of the same eclectic spirit, musicians for whom borrowing and adapting ideas and methods they had discovered in the musical worlds of jazz, classical, and folk was merely standard operating procedure.

By doing these things—by dressing as they liked, investigating alternatives to traditional views, and disregarding traditional artistic standards—the hippies of the '60s declared a kind of independence from cultural norms. In effect, they announced to all around them, all who would hear them, that individuals should not be bound by cultural rules, that every individual should adopt the motto Do Your Own Thing.

In effect, the revolution fashioned by the counterculture was a revolution in support of, a revolution in praise of, *decadence.*

13

The Decay of Authority

Decadence is one of those words that are ubiquitous and ambiguous, commonplace and obscure, all at the same time. Everyone knows what it means—just ask around, if you need any reassurance on that point—yet hardly anyone seems really to understand it.

Everyone knows, for example, that the word *decadence* refers to an overall condition of decay or decline, and that when we describe a civilization, or a period in the history of a civilization, as "decadent" we mean that the society or era of which we are speaking is no more than a pale, tired echo of some earlier society, some previous era, of enormously greater vitality and excellence.

Everyone knows, too, that there are certain particular periods in the history of certain particular civilizations which have been called "decadent" so persistently for so long by so many people that they have come to exemplify what "decadence" is all about. The history of Rome between 200 C.E. and 500 C.E. is one such

101

classic touchstone of "decadence." Another, drawn from more recent history, is the period between 1880 and 1905 in Paris and London. Yet another is the period between the end of World War I and the beginning of the Great Depression in Paris and New York.

The problem with this conventional understanding of decadence is that it won't bear close examination. Take a close look at the Gay Nineties and the Roaring Twenties, for example, and ask yourself exactly what was in decline in those periods. Where, precisely, was the decay? In what specific respects could these eras be said to be lacking in the vitality and excellence that had characterized earlier times?

Ordinarily, we judge the overall vitality and excellence of any given civilization (or any particular period in the history of a given civilization) by how much vitality and excellence the people of that civilization display in those fields of human endeavor which characteristically reach their highest stages of development only among *civilized* human beings, that is, among human beings who live in complex societies. In other words, we tend to judge the vitality and excellence of societies by the vitality and excellence of the scientific, technological, and artistic work performed by the people who make them up.

But it would be preposterous to maintain that science and technology entered upon a period of decline around the turn of the last century. For the years between 1880 and 1905 saw not only the invention of the airplane, the automobile, the motion picture, radio, and color photography, but also the discovery of radium and the first formulations of the theories of quantum mechanics and relativity which have revolutionized modern physics.

Nor was the science of healing in any sort of decline during the Gay Nineties. It was during the fin de siècle that physicians first developed and learned to use the X-ray, a vaccine effective against rabies, and workable techniques of both local and spinal anaesthesia. It was also at this time that other healing professionals first began working out and enunciating both the theory and the practical methods of a new discipline of healing which they called *chiropractic.*

And as for the arts . . . need it be mentioned that the last two decades of the nineteenth century and the first decade of the twentieth are deservedly world famous for the very vitality and excellence—the *uncommon* vitality and excellence—of the literature, the painting and drawing, and the music created during their passage? It is only necessary to invoke the names of a handful of the artists and artistic movements that flourished at that time—Wilde, James, Twain, Debussy, Mahler, Whistler, Beardsley, symbolism, impressionism—and the point is irrefutably made.

Not that the selfsame point is any more difficult to make with respect to the legendary 1920s. In the sciences, the discovery of penicillin and insulin and the invention of television, rocketry, the talking movie, FM radio, the elevator, and the iron lung; in the arts, the work of Sibelius, Ravel, Prokofiev, Gershwin, Hemingway, Faulkner, Picasso, and Magritte—who can describe all this as a pale, tired echo of some earlier period of true greatness while maintaining a straight face?

Yet, in fact, there *was* something in decline in Western Europe and North America during the 1890s and the 1920s, something whose decay really *did* play a central role in determining the basic, underlying character—the fundamental spirit—of each of those periods. In this sense, the 1890s and the 1920s *were* decadent. But the something of which I speak, the something whose decay made the 1890s and 1920s what they were, was not the creativity or the productivity or the skill with which the people of those eras did their work—the work on which every society must depend for whatever measure of wealth and whatever overall quality of life its members are able to enjoy.

No, the something I'm talking about is of an entirely different order. The French essasyist Paul Bourget seems to have been the first intellectual to put his finger on this something when he wrote in 1883 that, by traditional standards, "a society ought to be assimilated to an organism . . . [which] resolves itself into a federation of lesser organisms, which again resolve themselves into a federation of cells. The individual," in this conception of things, "is the social cell."

"If the energy of the cells becomes independent," Bourget wrote, "the organisms composing the total organism cease . . . to subordinate their energy to the total energy, and the anarchy which takes place constitutes the *decadence* of the whole."[34]

As we have seen, the chief means by which the energy of individuals is kept subordinate to the energy of society as a whole is the spontaneously ordered system of rules we call culture. Part of what it means to call a culture a spontaneous order is that the rules which make it up emerge gradually, over time, from the uncoordinated choices and actions of countless individuals; the only way any particular pattern of behavior can come to be recognized as the expression of a cultural rule or "norm" is by first becoming and then remaining over time the de facto norm in a society, the way most of the people in that society actually do behave under circumstances of some particular kind.

This means that the rules which constitute any particular culture, whatever they may be, will always be *traditional*. And, in any given culture, once a rule or norm has become traditional, it retains that status through the influence of *authority*. Tradition per se wields considerable authority. For a great many people, the mere fact that most of the other people who have lived where they are now living have chosen to live their lives in certain ways instead of others exerts a powerful influence: for surely (they tell themselves) all those people couldn't have been wrong; surely (they go on to assert) tradition is the means through which those who have lived before us pass down to us the lessons they have learned from their own experience about what works and what doesn't.

To persuade those not suitably impressed by the authority of tradition per se, culture relies on the authority of institutions and the individuals who speak for them. Every traditional idea, every traditional mode of behavior, winds up with at least one institution behind it. We have schools, associations, foundations, institutes, and scores and scores of less formally organized institutions avidly lined up behind every tiniest element of whatever happens to be the current conventional wisdom. If you won't believe X or Y merely because almost everyone else has believed it for a long, long time, then perhaps you'll listen to the testimony of the acknowledged experts of the National Academy of Sciences, or the American Medical Association, or the National Education Association, or the National Council of Churches, or the American Psychiatric Association, or the American Bar Association, or the National Association for the Advancement of Colored People, or the National Association of Broadcasters, or the National Association of Manufacturers, or the AFL-CIO. Or maybe you'll believe the consensus of opinion of the full professors of physics or chemistry or psychology or economics or literature or music at the nation's "leading" colleges and universities. Or maybe you'll believe the consensus of opinion of the editorialists and columnists and critics who write for the publications that "everyone acknowledges" are the "major," "influential," "important," "authoritative" newspapers and magazines in our society.

What happens during a decadent period, what *makes* any given period "decadent," is a general, overall decline in the influence of authority *as such*. The traditional rules, the traditional standards, are not cancelled; they go on obtaining. The traditional authorities go right on exercising influence. But, across the board, the perceived cost of deviating from tradition, ignoring the conventional wisdom, flying in the face of authority, is reduced. Where, before, the influence of traditional authority had been perceived as so powerful that to defy it in even the smallest way was to invite personally disastrous consequences, now, by contrast, it seems, if not exactly safe, then at least a great deal safer, to go one's own, nonconformist way.

Of course, different people react differently to this general perception of a loosening of the traditional rules and a reduction in the severity of the consequences for those who choose not to follow them. Please understand me. I am *not* saying that in decadent periods the majority of people suddenly decide to fly in the face of the cultural norms they have grown up observing. In decadent periods, the overwhelming majority of people go right on living their lives according to the dictates of tradition and authority, just as they do during what, for lack of a better term, I shall call *authoritarian* (which is to say, normal) periods.

At any time in the history of any civilization, it is only a small minority of the population which is courageous—or foolish—enough to literally fly in the face of tradition and authority. What distinguishes a decadent period in the history of a civilization from an authoritarian period in the history of the same civilization is the fact that during a decadent period there is a significant increase in the size of a borderline group—those who, by and large, accept the conventional wisdom, but who disagree with it in regard to this or that specific. In an authoritarian period, these people will not indulge their inclination to defy tradition; they will perceive the cost as too high. In a decadent period, many more of the people in this borderline group will indulge themselves. They will go on living their lives conventionally in almost every way. But they will permit themselves the courage of their true convictions in that one way in which, in their heart of hearts, they differ.

Still others inhabit a different sort of borderline group during the authoritarian periods in any particular society's history. These others don't really disagree with any of tradition's prescriptions for how they should live their lives; their secret heresy is that they can't really summon what seems to them to be the expected outrage at those of their fellows who *don't* follow the prescriptions. In authoritarian periods, these people suppress and conceal their live-and-let-live attitudes. In decadent periods, they indulge them. They go on living their own lives in a traditional manner, but they refrain from hassling those of their neighbors who choose to do otherwise.

Certain others—and they are typically quite numerous— react strongly to the general loosening of traditional rules and traditional sanctions for violating the rules which characterize decadent periods by finding ways to hew even more closely to these rules and sanctions and to dramatize their decision to do so, and, sometimes, if possible, to find political ways to force everyone else to follow their lead. It was reactionaries of this kind, made frantic by the deviations from tradition they saw all around them, who managed, by means of expert political organization and dedicated concentration of their full energy on a single political issue, to impose nationwide prohibition of alcoholic beverages on the United States at a time when all the prevalent cultural trends were in a precisely contrary direction—in the direction of *decadence,* which is to say, the direction of individual freedom from the dictates of traditional authority.

In a decadent period, those rebellious individuals who would rebel under any circumstances find that their chosen path creates fewer difficulties for them than it would under ordinary circumstances. Some of them even manage to attain a certain eminence, a certain *influence,* paradoxical as it may seem, on the strength of their failure to conform to what is expected of them. And, as we have seen, a great many of those who would, in an authoritarian period, suppress their areas of disagreement with the conventional wisdom, choose instead to pursue their heresies, while leading otherwise conventional lives. Still others, as we have seen—a multitude of others—greet such heresies with tolerance, while conforming themselves.

The result is an enormous increase in creativity. All genuinely *new* ideas are, inescapably, untraditional ideas. In an atmosphere in which it is unsafe to challenge whatever happens to be the prevailing orthodoxy, very little is invented or discovered. Is it not obvious that it is only in an environment in which the serious investigator feels free to dare to defy the conventional wisdom that there is *any chance at all* of learning anything genuinely *new*?

On the other hand, it is also true that one reason the conventional wisdom *is* the conventional wisdom is that it has proved itself workable over time. The general loosening of the rules and the traditional sanctions for breaking the rules which characterizes periods of cultural decadence leads to widespread experimentation with all sorts of theories which, in normal, authoritarian times, would be regarded as foolish, silly, "off the wall," already discredited, or for some other reason(s) unworthy of investigation. And, in fact, most such theories *are* unworthy, just as the conventional wisdom would have us believe.

This is the reason why, when we contemplate periods like the 1890s and the 1920s, we see such an incredible surge of creativity and invention in both the arts and the sciences, side by side with an equally incredible surge of intellectual, artistic, and scientific folly. This is why we see the invention of radio and television side by side with a vogue for spiritualism, Ouija boards, and numerology. This is why we see the discovery of penicillin and insulin side by side with the growth of psychoanalysis and homeopathy. This is why we see the emergence of relativity theory and quantum mechanics side by side with the "discovery" of Christian Science and the Book of Mormon. The common denominator is not accuracy or truth, but *decadence,* the overall decay of the influence of traditional authority.

This decay paves the way for unconventional ideas in every sphere of human activity and endeavor. In education, for example, it is no accident that the radically unconventional theories of Maria Montessori first gained currency in Europe in the 1890s and scored their first great successes in America in the 1920s. Nor is it mere coincidence that made the '90s the age of ragtime and the '20s the "Jazz Age": this new American music could only have been created in times when musicians could safely disregard traditional musical categories and traditional rules of musical composition and performance.

The same is true of that later musical hybrid known as rock and roll. Rock first came into being in the 1950s, when certain enterprising musicians began freely combining techniques borrowed from white country music with still other techniques borrowed from black rhythm and blues—in flagrant defiance of tradition. At that time, tradition not only demanded that traditional distinctions between musical styles be strictly respected—that traditionally separate categories of music remain separate and not be combined; it demanded that these two types of music in particular be kept absolutely apart, no matter what the cost.

Traditionally, they had been—just as the races themselves, white and black, had been. White country musicians and black rhythm and blues musicians not only didn't play each other's music, they didn't perform in the same clubs and concert halls, and they didn't record for the same record companies; nor were their records sold in the same stores or played on the same radio stations. Those were the rules.

When musicians like Elvis Presley, Jerry Lee Lewis, Bill Haley, and Chuck Berry, and disc jockeys like Alan Freed, began breaking those rules, they brought a full-fledged national scandal down on their heads. They ran into a solid wall of indignation and resistance. And though the new musical style they had pioneered did bring about some important changes in the traditional world of American popular music even during those early years, it fell far short of transforming that world. The cultural influence of traditional musical authority was still too powerful.

Then, a little less than a decade later, the nation erupted in cultural revolution. Millions of youthful rebels began proclaiming—and clearly demonstrating—their intention to "do their own thing," whether it met with the approval of traditional authority or not. And the influence of traditional authority in our society went into a decline from which it has still not recovered.

In this new atmosphere, the new music which had faced such an uphill struggle only a few years before not only came into its own, it swept through the world of American popular music like a tidal wave, transforming everything in its path. Within ten years, rock and roll of one kind or another (for the new music went right on growing and changing and evolving, eclectically borrowing ideas and techniques from every other musical style you could imagine, utterly without regard for traditional categories and distinctions and rules) had virtually *become* American popular music. No other kind of music could even approach its popularity. It sometimes seemed as though no other kind of music even existed any more. It was the story of the triumph of jazz during the 1890s and 1920s all over again, only more so.

Nor was this the only respect in which the new decadent period resembled those two earlier ones. In the 1890s and the 1920s, the decay of authority led to widespread questioning of traditional sex roles and traditional restrictions on sexual activity and to widespread experimentation with alternatives. The same thing happened again in the 1960s.

In the 1890s and the 1920s, the decay of authority led to the formation of a mass movement designed to challenge traditional conceptions of the status of women in society. The same thing happened again in the 1960s.

In the 1890s and the 1920s, the decay of authority led to a rapid proliferation of "isms"—socialism, anarchism, vegetarianism, Buddhism, Hinduism, communism, occultism, nudism, aestheticism, and a host of others—whose only common denominator was deviation from the conventional wisdom of the time. The same thing happened again in the 1960s.

In the 1890s and the 1920s, the decay of authority paved the way for a new and ferociously candid iconoclasm in print. And the same thing happened again in the 1960s. Consider a few examples, chosen at random from the annals of a single nation, our own. The 1890s saw the publication of such works as Ambrose Bierce's *Devil's Dictionary,* and *The Anatomy of Negation,* a history of antitheism by one Edgar Saltus, who, when asked by a reporter to name his favorite character in fiction, is said to have replied, "God." The 1920s was the heyday of that most notorious of all literary scofflaws, H. L. Mencken. And it was during the 1960s that writers like Thomas Szasz (in *The Myth of Mental Illness*) and R. D. Laing (in *The Politics of Experience*) scored major successes by questioning the conventional wisdom regarding psychology and psychiatry, all the while that still other writers—Paul Goodman, John Holt, Ivan Illich—were becoming famous by challenging the conventional wisdom regarding education.

Moreover, like the 1890s and the 1920s, the decadent era that began in the 1960s has witnessed an altogether extraordinary outpouring of creativity in the sciences and the arts. In the sciences, think of the electronics and computer revolutions of the past few decades, and of such medical advances as the development of organ-transplant surgery, open-heart surgery, the "bypass" operation, and the artificial heart. In the arts, think not only of the filmmakers who have learned to exploit the artistic potentialities of the aforementioned computer, but also of the musical pioneers—men like Vangelis, Edgar Froese, and Mike Oldfield—who began working in the 1960s to explore and exploit the seemingly limitless potentialities of the first genuinely *new* musical instrument in nearly a century, the synthesizer. Think, too, of the incredible renaissance of literary creativity, especially in America, which has occurred over the past thirty-five years.

Part Two

The Shape of Things to Come

14

Degeneration Revisited

Of course, not everything about decadence is admirable and desirable. There is a downside to it as well. Look around you: are not our families, our cities, our standards of public civility all going to hell in a handbasket? Books that say as much have been issuing from the publisher-infested canyons of Manhattan over the past two decades in a steady stream. Twenty years ago, it was Christopher Lasch sounding the alarm, fifteen years ago it was Letty Cottin Pogrebin, five years ago it was William A. Henry III. But the message is, at bottom, always the same—as is the brief vogue it periodically touches off in the intellectual weeklies, fortnightlies, and monthlies (to say nothing of the more intellectually pretentious television programs). Each time it arises, this brief frenzy of cultural doomsaying tells us more about the habits of mind—and the educational deficiencies—of the reading public than it does about the actual value and relevance of the ideas that have set that public all aflutter.

Consider the case of Christopher Lasch. It will be difficult,

115

perhaps, for younger readers to imagine the intensity of the furor Lasch stirred up in November 1978 when he published what would turn out to be his most famous book, *The Culture of Narcissism: American Life in an Age of Diminishing Expectations.*[35] For more than a year thereafter—until well into 1980—the editorial, opinion, and book columns of the more intelligent and influential newspapers were full of little else. Lasch was also in the major magazines—*Time, Newsweek,* the *New Republic, Commentary,* the *Nation.* Lasch was on television. Lasch was everywhere, preaching his gospel that our culture was suffering and dying from pathological narcissism. Yet, perversely, all this attention to Lasch's argument only really succeeded in establishing one rather odd but inescapable conclusion: that Max Nordau and his once-infamous works had been truly and completely forgotten.

Max Nordau (1849–1923) was a Jewish-Hungarian physician, author, and Zionist. He grew up in Budapest, attended college and medical school there, and practiced medicine and journalism there for a few years before moving to Paris, where he devoted several years to postgraduate study in medicine, engaged in further periodical writing, and eventually resumed his medical practice.

It was during his Paris years (he spent most of his last years in a kind of self-imposed exile in Madrid) that he achieved international notoriety through his books. (He eventually became famous enough that in 1903 he survived an assassination attempt spurred by his Zionist activities.) His first important books began appearing during the 1880s: *Conventional Lies of Our Civilization* (1883), *Paradoxes* (1885), and *The Sickness of the Century* (1887). By 1892, when his magnum opus, *Degeneration,* was published, he had become well enough established that his books were routinely brought out in both French and English as well as in their original German.[36]

Degeneration made an enormous splash. One might say that

it was *The Culture of Narcissism* of its time. It was easily the most influential of the many extended essays in social criticism which were being published during the last years of the last century. It was the trans-Atlantic debate over *Degeneration* that occasioned the first appearance in American print of George Bernard Shaw, who replied to Nordau at length in an essay called "The Sanity of Art" in the July 27, 1895 issue of Benjamin R. Tucker's anarchist publication, *Liberty*.

But *Degeneration* is famous no longer. In one of the few references to it which I have been able to find in any contemporary piece of writing, Richard Gilman (in his *Decadence: The Strange Life of an Epithet,* 1979) dismisses it as "a shabby, disreputable, but well-known 1898 tome," and implicitly calls into question his own assertion of its great fame by not even getting its publication date right. In some ways, as we shall see, Nordau's oblivion is well deserved. Yet if he had been more widely known among readers two decades ago, those readers might not have showered encomia upon such a book as *The Culture of Narcissism*—a book which is remarkable chiefly for its highly unimaginative (if, perhaps, unintended) echoing of *Degeneration.* Indeed, so obvious is this echoing to anyone familiar with Nordau's work that the failure of any of the dozens of journalists and critics and publicists who invested so much ink and airtime in *The Culture of Narcissism* twenty years ago to even mention its striking similarity to the earlier book must, as I have said, be taken in itself as evidence of the extent to which Nordau has been forgotten. Consider the facts.

Nordau was a student of Cesare Lombroso, the Italian psychiatrist who "discovered" not only that anti-Semitism is a mental illness, but also that criminals are genetic "degenerates" who can be identified by certain physical and mental "stigmata" of "atavism." Lasch was a student of Lombroso's frankly admiring contemporary, Sigmund Freud, the Viennese psychiatrist who "discovered" that, as Vladimir Nabokov has neatly summed it up, "all mental woes can be cured by a daily application of old Greek myths to [the] private parts." Nordau announces at the beginning of *Degeneration* that

> the disposition of the times is curiously confused, a compound of feverish restlessness and blunted discouragement, of fearful presage and hang-dog renunciation. The prevalent feeling is that of imminent perdition and extinction. *Fin-de-siècle* is at once a confession and a complaint. The old Northern faith contained the fearsome doctrine of the Dusk of the Gods. In our days there have arisen in more highly-developed minds vague qualms of a Dusk of the Nations, in which all suns and all stars are gradually waning, and mankind with all its institutions and creations is perishing in the midst of a dying world. (p. 2)

Lasch announces at the beginning of *The Culture of Narcissism* that

> as the twentieth century approaches its end, the conviction grows that many other things are ending too. Storm warnings, portents, hints of catastrophe haunt our times. The 'sense of an ending' which has given shape to so much of twentieth-century literature, now pervades the popular imagination as well. . . . The question of whether the world will end in fire or in ice, with a bang or a whimper, no longer interests artists alone. Impending disaster has become an everyday concern, so commonplace and familiar that nobody any longer gives much thought to how disaster might be averted. (pp. 3–4)

Nordau believes that it is a kind of sickness which has brought us to this pass. "The physician," he writes,

> especially if he have devoted himself to the special study of nervous and mental maladies, recognizes at a glance, in the *fin-de-siècle* disposition, in the tendencies of contemporary art and poetry, in the life and conduct of the men who write mystic, symbolic and "decadent" works, and the attitude taken by their admirers in the tastes and aesthetic instincts of fashionable society, the confluence of two well-defined conditions of disease, with which he is quite familiar, viz. degeneration (degeneracy) and hysteria, of which the minor stages are designated as neurasthenia. (p. 15)

Lasch, too, sees disease as the underlying source of our cultural malaise: specifically "the character traits associated with pathological narcissism, which in less extreme form appear in such profusion in the everyday life of our age . . ." (p. 35).

"In the clinical literature," he writes, "narcissism has come to be recognized as an important element in the so-called character disorders that have absorbed much of the clinical attention once given to hysteria and obsessional neuroses."

Both Nordau and Lasch argue that the sickness of an age manifests itself not only in the type of pathological personality which is most common during that age, but also in the normal, more or less healthy personality of the average person of that age. "The difference between disease and health is not one of kind, but of quantity," says Nordau. "Pathology represents a heightened version of normality," says Lasch (p. 175). And "every society reproduces its culture—its norms, its underlying assumptions, its modes of organizing experience," whether these norms, assumptions, and modes are healthy or not, "in the individual, in the form of personality. As Durkheim said, personality is the individual socialized" (p. 34).

And what is this fin-de-siècle personality—whether normal or pathological—all about? Mainly it is about selfishness, "a love of self," as Nordau puts it,

> never met with in a sane person in anything like the same degree. The hysterical person's own "I" towers up before his inner vision, and so completely fills his mental horizon that it conceals the whole of the remaining universe. He cannot endure that others should ignore him. He desires to be as important to his fellow men as he is to himself. (p. 26)

And this *ego-mania,* as Nordau calls it, this *narcissism,* as Lasch calls it, is nowhere more on display than in the literature of the age. Lasch writes of "the increasing interpenetration of fiction, journalism, and autobiography," and the fact that "instead

of fictionalizing personal material or otherwise reordering it,"
serious writers have "taken to presenting it undigested" and to
including in their books "the kind of spurious confession whose
only claim to the reader's attention is that it describes events of
immediate interest to the author" (pp. 17–18). As Lasch sees it,
any author of such a confessional piece "seeks not to provide an
objective account of a representative piece of reality but to
seduce others into giving him their attention, acclaim, or sym-
pathy and thus to shore up his faltering sense of self" (p. 21).

Nordau agrees entirely. "Formerly," he writes, "it was the
custom to utilize . . . excursions into all possible fields of discussion as articles for newspapers or monthly periodicals, and after-
wards to collect them in book form. But experience has taught us
that the public does not exhibit much interest in these collections
of essays." Accordingly, authors on the make—the French novelist J. K. Huysmans is Nordau's central example—have con-
cocted a new literary form: a novel which consists of nothing but
"the description of a human being, with his intellectual life, and
his monotonous, scarcely modulated external destinies." This
form demands no skill as a plotwright or storyteller, but "gives
the author a pretext for expressing his own ideas on all possible
subjects." Nordau complains that "M. Huysmans and his school"
have transformed "the novel from an epic poem in prose into a
hybrid mixture of the *Essays* of Montaigne, of [the] *Parerga et
Paralipomena* [literally "By-products and Leavings"—the mis-
cellaneous essays] of Schopenhauer, and the effusions in the
diary of a girl at boarding school" (pp. 310–11).

Not only is the narcissistic personality, the personality of the
egomaniac, fervently devoted to exhibitionism; it is elitist as
well. The narcissist relies on others to make him the center of
attention, but he despises them nevertheless. "The narcissist,"
says Lasch,

> divides society into two groups: the rich, great and famous on the
> one hand and the common herd on the other. Narcissistic patients,

according to Otto Kernberg, "are afraid of not belonging to the company of the great, rich and powerful, and of belonging instead to the 'mediocre,' by which they mean worthless and despicable rather than 'average' in the ordinary sense of the term." (p. 84)

The degenerate, says Nordau, "is fain to despise the vulgar herd for the dullness and narrowness of their minds" (p. 19).

Both Nordau and Lasch deny that the narcissistic, exhibitionistic, self-preoccupation they have described is in any sense the same thing as simple selfishness or egoism. "Egoism," Nordau writes,

> is a lack of amiability, a defect in education, perhaps a fault of character, a proof of insufficiently developed morality, but it is not a disease. The egoist is quite able to look after himself in life, and hold his place in society. . . . The ego-maniac, on the contrary, is an invalid who does not see things as they are, does not understand the world, and cannot take up a right attitude towards it. (p. 243)

Lasch argues that "men have always been selfish," and asserts that "narcissism has more in common with self-hatred than with self-admiration," because it leads ineluctably to self-defeating or self-destructive behavior (p. 31).

Interestingly, both Nordau's ego-maniac and Lasch's narcissist are archconsumers. "A stigma of degeneration," Nordau writes, is

> "oniomania" or "buying craze." This is not to be confounded with the desire for buying which possesses those who are in the first stage of general paralysis. The purchases of these persons are due to their delusion as to their own greatness. They lay in great supplies because they fancy themselves millionaires. The oniomaniac, on the contrary, neither buys enormous quantities of one and the same thing, nor is the price a matter of indifference to him as with the paralytic. He is simply unable to pass by any lumber without feeling an impulse to acquire it. (p. 27)

Similarly, Lasch writes of the narcissist:

> Acquisitive in the sense that his cravings have no limits, he does not
> accumulate goods and provisions against the future, in the manner of
> the acquisitive individualist of nineteenth-century political economy,
> but demands immediate gratification and lives in a state of restless,
> perpetually unsatisfied desire. (p. xvi)

It would be possible to go on like this for many more pages than I have filled already, but the point is made. Christopher Lasch's much touted, much praised *Culture of Narcissism* is little more than an updated rewrite of Max Nordau's discredited and forgotten *Degeneration*. The two books agree not only in their fundamental ideas, but even in small details of their arguments and in their illustrative examples. Nordau explains that the degenerate cultivates forbidden vices and becomes a seeker of thrills at any cost because his degeneration has brought with it a blunted sensitivity to stimuli of all kinds, and he needs intense experiences if he is to feel anything at all; Lasch describes the attempt of the narcissist to "cultivate more vivid experiences, . . . beat sluggish flesh to life, . . . revive jaded appetites" (p. 11). Nordau likens the ego-maniac to "a mental Robinson Crusoe, who in his imagination lives alone on an island, and is at the same time a weak creature, powerless to govern himself" (p. 259). Lasch likens the nineteenth-century rugged individualist who saw the world "as an empty wilderness to be shaped to his own design" to Robinson Crusoe, and asserts that the twentieth-century narcissist more closely resembles Moll Flanders (p. 53).

It is easy, of course, to dismiss Nordau entirely, merely by discrediting the ideas of Lombroso on which his analysis rests. Similarly, it is easy to dismiss Lasch by discrediting the ideas of Freud on which his analysis rests—for example, by saying sweepingly as Sir Peter Medawar does that "psychoanalytic theory is the most stupendous intellectual confidence trick of the twentieth century." But this is not only too easy, it is also unnecessary. There are other grounds aplenty for dismissing *The Culture of Narcissism,* not the least of which is its internal incoherence. Nor does one have to venture far into the book before one stumbles over this particular fault time and time again.

Lasch tells us near the beginning of his first chapter that Americans are in "retreat from politics" and have turned their attention "to purely personal preoccupations. Having no hope of improving their lives in any of the ways that matter, people have convinced themselves that what matters is psychic self-improvement" (p. 4). Yet only a few pages earlier, in his preface, he has written that "the 'flight from politics,' as it appears to the managerial and political elite, may signify the citizen's growing unwillingness to take part in the political system as a consumer of prefabricated spectacles. It may signify, in other words, not a retreat from politics at all but the beginnings of a general political revolt" (p. 15). And a little later, near the end of chapter 1, he faults fellow culture critic Edwin Schur for "setting up an over-simplified opposition between 'real' issues and personal issues" and for ignoring "the fact that social questions inevitably present themselves also as personal ones" (p. 26).

Which is it? one wonders. Are Americans in retreat from politics or brewing a revolution? Are they substituting a concern with the self for their old concern with the polity, or have they begun considering the previously overlooked personal dimension of their old social concerns? No, Christopher Lasch didn't do a particularly good job of catching inconsistencies and contradictions when he edited and strung together into a book what had originally been a series of more or less discrete magazine articles.

So why then did *The Culture of Narcissism,* unimpressive, uncreative rehash that it is, cause all that intellectual and cultural turmoil when it first came out, just before the penultimate decade of our century was about to get under way? More than anything else, it was the fact that the book echoed and amplified a fear already widespread in the American population—a fear of the future, of the shape of things to come. If, as seemed apparent,

American society was crumbling all around them, if it was breaking up into its constituent individuals and into only such likeminded bands as those individuals freely chose to join or associate with, then . . . what lay ahead? Would it be as William Butler Yeats had foreseen? When the center could no longer hold, would "mere anarchy" be "loosed upon the world"?

15

All in the Family

When people fear what the future might bring, their first and most powerful fear is usually for their families. As Christopher Lasch observed only a few years before the publication of *The Culture of Narcissism,* the family, for most of us, is a *Haven in a Heartless World,* a place where we can retire for rest and succor in the face of the relentless demands and challenges the outside world throws at us on a daily basis. And if our families themselves are imperiled by forces at work in society at large, forces over which we have no control, what then? Surely, readers of the late 1970s must have felt, Christopher Lasch had been right on target when he subtitled his second most famous book "The Family Besieged."

Certainly other writers of the period thought so. As the 1980s unfolded, dozens of them aggressively jumped on Lasch's bandwagon, making as much hay as they could muster with that self-same fear. "The family is a hot issue," wrote Letty Cottin Pogrebin, longtime feminist and one of the founding editors of *Ms.* magazine, in her book *Family Politics,* published in 1983.

Judging by the proliferation of magazine cover stories, television features, talk show discussions, academic research, and public policy discourse being devoted to the state of the American family, it seems safe to say that what civil rights and Vietnam were to the Sixties, and women's rights and the environment were to the Seventies, family issues have become to the Eighties.[37]

Pogrebin was probably overstating her case a little, but not by much. The evidence in support of her contention was to be found not only in the magazine articles, academic publications, and TV shows to which she alluded, but also in the pages of the many books on marriage and family matters that were published in the early 1980s (and have continued to be published in an unremitting stream ever since).

In one of these books, *What's Happening to the American Family?* (1981), "communitarian" sociologist Sar Levitan and his colleague Richard Belous write, "Marriage and family appear to have fallen on hard times," and the resulting

sense of something falling apart has even reached the White House. ... Both Democratic and Republican Presidents have foreseen disturbing omens in current family trends. The Carter administration launched a nationwide White House Conference on Families in an effort to cope with these problems. Not to be outdone, Ronald Reagan proclaimed, upon accepting the Republican nomination, that his administration would be a crusade to revitalize American institutions. The first institution on his list was the family.[38]

As we know, White House concern for the vitality of the family did not end with the Reagan and Bush administrations. The two Clinton administrations of the 1990s have kept the ball rolling with a vengeance. And over on Capitol Hill, a constantly changing group of predominantly Republican lawmakers has been agonizing over the plight of the family ever since 1979, when the first version of the Family Protection Act was proposed to set things right again by moving "to preserve the integrity of the American family, to foster and protect the viability of American family life . . . and to promote the virtues of the family."

The problem is that what the Moral Majoritarians and hidebound traditionalists who have pushed for legislation of this kind for the past two decades really mean when they talk about "the family" is the so-called traditional family: a breadwinning father, a full-time housewife mother, and one or more children. But only about one American household in four these days is inhabited by such a family. Most American households are now occupied by untraditional families, by childless couples, or by single individuals living alone.

According to most partisans of "save the family" legislation, what lies at the heart of the current crisis of the American family is precisely the fact that this "traditional" family—the household type that (they contend) has always been the norm in America—has lately begun eroding away, mostly in response to certain meddlesome policies of the federal government. It is true, of course, that certain recent federal programs have created incentives to break up "traditional" families—the welfare rules, for example, that reward an unemployed father for deserting his family. Yet in point of fact, the decline of the "traditional" family did not begin a mere few decades ago with the birth of these particular types of federal meddling. It began long, long before.

"The family, in its old sense," wrote a contributor to the *Boston Quarterly Review* of October 1859, "is disappearing from our land, and not only our free institutions are threatened but the very existence of society is endangered." Yet Jonathan Gathorne-Hardy reports in his book *Marriage, Love, Sex and Divorce* (1981) that this very same same state of affairs existed more than 150 years before in Stuart England, where many of the original American colonists came from. "Far from stable," writes Gathorne-Hardy, the family in seventeenth-century Britain

was in a state of "collapse" which it has not yet reached even in America. At Clayworth (one of the parishes where evidence over time exists) in 1688, 39 percent of marriages were with a partner married before; 13 percent were second marriages, 3 percent were third marriages, 4 percent were fourth and one person had had five previous partners. From other sources one can gauge that approximately one-third of all marriages in Stuart England were second marriages or more.[39]

Of course, the reasons for marital termination were different in those days. "Death played the part then that divorce does now," Gathorne-Hardy notes. And "one can speculate that, if the same conditions existed today and if death struck by chance as often, then one-third of the marriages which today solve their difficulties by divorce would have solved them by death" (p. 293).

"The idea that the instability of modern Western marriage, all the divorcing and splitting and affairs, somehow means that society is less stable, is not true," Gathorne-Hardy concludes.

> The institutions in the old world were expedients to provide an illusion of permanence in a world which was impermanent and insecure. They were therefore talked and written about as permanent to such an extent that we have come to believe it. The evidence, however, is that they were not. (pp. 294–95)

All in all, "we are just as stable as the past."

Is more evidence needed? Very well. "In the 1860s," Richard Sennett wrote in 1977 in *The Fall of Public Man,*

> social workers in both London and Paris were . . . worrying about the demoralization of the poor, and linking that demoralization to the family conditions in which the poor lived. In the 1860s, as in the 1960s, a "broken home" was usually taken to be the specific culprit, again with a female as the usual head of the household.[40]

Levitan and Belous, in *What's Happening to the American Family?* sum the matter up:

> marital disruption was also a problem in the "good old days," even though its causes have shifted. With vast improvements in health,

plunging death rates for all ages counterbalanced increases in the divorce rate during this century to such a degree that the rate of marital disruption for all causes was fairly stable until 1970.[41]

Levitan and Belous remind us also that nineteenth-century America "was full of experimental communities that explored new family forms," communities like John Humphrey Noyes's Oneida, which did away with traditional marriage altogether on the grounds that it was contrary to human nature. But, Levitan and Belous comment, even when it has been

> granted that alternative family structures have always existed, it has been argued that a growing number of individuals are availing them-selves of these opportunities. Even this point is highly debatable. For example, while there has been a vast increase in the reported number of couples living together without the blessings of state or church, it is quite difficult to know how much of this shift is really a new trend. *With diminished social pressures to follow any one pattern* a good portion of the reported increase in this behavior may represent only the increased willingness of people to be open about what has always taken place. "Swinging" is probably one of the oldest indoor sports known to humanity, as even a casual reader of the Bible would easily find, and not all of the participants were villains. What may be new is the willingness on the part of the players to publicly extol its virtues to the multitudes." (Emphasis added)[42]

Johns Hopkins University sociologist Andrew Cherlin, author of *Marriage, Divorce, Remarriage* (1981), carries this line of thinking to its obvious conclusion by arguing that what we see around us today, what the Moral Majoritarians decry as "the crisis of the family," is in fact the norm in American life, the norm from which our national experience during the hallowed 1950s was a unique deviation. "The birthrate has been declining since the 1820s," Cherlin writes,

> the divorce rate has been climbing since at least the Civil War, and over the last half century a growing number of married women have taken paying jobs. Thus, many of the changes we witnessed in family

life in the 1960s and 1970s were a continuation of long-term trends that have been with us for generations.

"The only exception occurred during the late 1940s and the 1950s," Cherlin continues.

> After World War II, Americans raised during the austerity of the Depression and the war entered adulthood at a time of sustained prosperity. The sudden turnabout in their fortunes led them to marry earlier and have more children than any generation before or since in this century. Because many of us were either parents or children in the baby-boom years following the war, we tend to think nostalgically that the 1950s typify the way twentieth century families used to be. But the patterns of marriage and childbearing in the 1950s were a historical aberration: the patterns of the 1960s and 1970s better fit the long-term trends.[43]

What is the meaning of these long-term trends? What is their cause? If they have been with us since the last century it would seem obvious that they can hardly be attributed to the interventions of big government and the welfare state. In fact, there is evidence to suggest that even in recent years government interventions have been only a minor factor in accelerating these trends. It is common knowledge, for example, that the federal welfare program known as Aid to Families with Dependent Children encourages the formation of single-parent households, commonly consisting of unmarried, unskilled, unemployed women and their children. Yet Levitan and Belous report that, as of 1981, "most of the increase in female headed households is accounted for by childless women who are ineligible for public assistance benefits."[44]

These childless women are forming their own self-headed households, not because of some action of some government, *but because that is how they choose to live their lives.* Cherlin refers to "the growing likelihood that unmarried individuals will choose to maintain their own households rather than live with kin" as "perhaps the most important [change that has] affected the composition of households." He writes:

> It used to be common . . . for a woman to move back to her parent's home after she separated from her husband, but today separated and divorced women are much more likely to set up their own households. Never-married young adults, whose members have been increasing, are less likely to remain at home until they marry than they were twenty years ago. Similarly, more older, widowed people are living by themselves rather than moving in with their children. It may be that the preferences of unmarried adults concerning living arrangements have changed. I suspect, however, that most unmarried adults always have preferred to live independently, only today they are more likely to have the financial resources to do so.[45]

It might also be argued, of course, that most married adults always have preferred to remain married only when they found their marriages personally satisfying but are more likely today to have the financial resources and to live in the decadent, "do your own thing" environment which can lend reality to the desire to exercise such a preference. "Many of the traditional reasons why people got married and stayed married are less compelling today," Cherlin writes.

> The greater economic independence of women means that marriage is less necessary as an economic partnership, as a common enterprise that creates a joint product neither partner could produce alone. And as the success of the economic enterprise becomes less crucial to husbands and wives, their personal satisfaction with their marriage becomes relatively more important. Consequently, it seems to me, husbands and wives are more likely today than in the past to evaluate their marriage primarily according to how well it satisfies their individual emotional needs. If their evaluation on these terms is unfavorable, they are likely to turn to divorce and then, perhaps, to another marriage.[46]

The conclusion seems inescapable. People used to have children because they felt they had to; there was no acceptable alternative. They used to get married and stay married because they had to. And once they had become old and feeble they used to live with their children and rely upon them for their support because they had to. Once they no longer had to do these things, they stopped doing them.

This is, says Cherlin,

> the way in which the United States—and, indeed, every advanced industrial society—has developed. As we moved from a rural, agricultural society to an urban, industrial one, the economic value of children declined and people had fewer of them. As the production of goods and services shifted from the home to the factory or the office, women were drawn into the labor market, thereby becoming more independent of men. And as the school, the hospital and the old-age home took over many of the functions family members used to perform for each other, men and women found it progressively easier to live nontraditional family lives.[47]

Should it surprise anyone—particularly in a decadent period —that people have taken advantage of this newfound opportunity? Does it really come as a surprise even to the prating Bible thumpers of the Moral Majority to learn that the "traditional" nuclear family is not the best of all possible worlds for everyone?

"When I can no longer bear to think of the victims of broken homes," says Peter De Vries, "I begin to think of the victims of intact ones." And the latter are legion. "A high incidence of violence within the family has come to light in recent years," wrote Levitan and Belous nearly two decades ago (and, as we all know, studies in more recent years have found the selfsame high incidence).

> Almost 1 million children may be neglected or abused each year, and as many as 2 million women may experience violence in the home. . . . The Office of Domestic Violence in the Department of Health and Human Services estimated that about one of four couples will undergo serious family violence during the course of a marriage or relationship. Roughly 25 percent of all homicides involve spouses

and 20 percent of all police deaths and 40 percent of police injuries occur when an officer responds to a "family violence" call.

Moreover, they report, "automobile accident cases still make up the majority of suits in court, but family-related cases are currently running a close second."[48]

Karen Lindsey, the avowedly leftist and feminist author of the 1981 book *Friends as Family,* paints an even grimmer picture. "As many as 60 percent of all married women are beaten at least once by their husbands," she writes. "And between 500,000 and one million elderly patients are abused each year by the adult offspring they live with."[49] The National Campaign for the Prevention of Child Abuse and Neglect estimates that "in up to 20 percent of American families, children are subjected to physical abuse, sexual abuse and neglect." And then there's the runaway problem. "An estimated 2 million youngsters run away from home every year," the *Los Angeles Times* reported in late November 1981, "and that rate is steadily increasing. While 15- and 16-year-olds account for nearly half the runaways, they range in age from 10 and 11 on up, and the national Runaway Switchboard reports serving children as young as 8 and 9."

If these kids run away, if their mothers seek divorces, if their grandparents choose to live by themselves, can anybody realistically contend that they have made these choices because an unholy alliance of secular humanists and godless communists has conspired against the "traditional family"? These people leave the family because in their homes familiarity has bred contempt and worse than contempt. "The family is the American fascism," said Paul Goodman. And for many in our society, that is precisely what it is.

For many others, myself included, the family is something else entirely. It is a way of life, and one which we feel we have freely chosen because of the various satisfactions it offers us. Why do we do it? Why do people form families? What are families for, anyway?

There are those—fundamentalist Christians, for example—who argue that such questions are pointless. We live in families because that's the way God set things up in the beginning, with Adam and Eve and Cain and Abel. That's all we know and all we need to know. Trying to figure out why God set it up that way is as foolish as trying to figure out the significance of the fact that the very first nuclear family in all of human history exploded into an act of violence that left one of its members dead at the hand of another of its members, even though violence on TV, rock music, secular humanism, and the federal government of the United States were not problems in the Garden of Eden.

But set these true believers aside for the moment: we'll be coming back to them soon enough. The conventional wisdom among most other students of the family as a social institution is that its purpose is economic and broadly cultural. On the one hand, it offers its members the easiest or most efficient way of getting a decent living. On the other, it provides its members, especially its child members, with practical training in the skills one needs to deal with other people in the outside world.

When life was mainly agricultural and the home was the workplace, families were large and typically included several generations. This assured an adequate number of able bodies to do the work, and it assured that those who had become too old and feeble to do any hard work would be available to look after those children who were still too small to do any hard work. And everyone benefited from the arrangement. The children and the old folks were obviously able to get a better living for themselves by living in a family than they could have got by themselves. And the able-bodied adults in their prime who might have done all right on their own also gained certain economic advantages by living in the family. Perhaps most important among these was the knowledge that in time of illness or temporary disability, there would be people to care for them and absorb the cost of their daily lives until they could work again. In this sense, the family was a source of security, an insurance policy.

But as the Industrial Revolution simultaneously raised per capita income and moved the population into cities, this kind of security became increasingly irrelevant. The home was no longer the sole workplace, so it was not advantageous to add members to the household, whether in the form of new children or aged relatives. Now that the remunerative work of the family was done outside the home, new additions were no longer added hands; they were added *costs*—parasites, if you will. On top of that, while space for additional people was cheap in the country, it was very expensive in the city. So people began living in smaller families, and the norm became parents and their children, but neither the parents' parents nor the children's children. The extended family had given way to the nuclear family.

Since that time, per capita income has continued to climb, and various institutions, some of them voluntary, some of them governmental (which is to say compulsory), have begun taking over many of the old functions of the family. You don't have to live in a family any longer to assure yourself of income during time of illness or temporary disability—all you have to do is buy an insurance policy or fill out the forms to qualify yourself for government disability payments. You no longer need your aged parent at home to watch the kids while you work—you can send the kids to a day-care center or a public school, and you can send the aged parent to an old folks' home. If your income is high enough you can pay strangers to do all the things for you that you used to get from family members. And if your income isn't high enough, you can probably get some extra money from the government to make it high enough.

For people who don't like the members of their biological families (and such people have been quite common ever since the days of Cain and Abel), the temptation to hire strangers and live alone is apparently great. Others who don't like the members of their biological families seem to feel a different temptation, however. They leave their biological families, but they don't hire strangers. Instead, they move in with other individuals and form surrogate families of various kinds.

These surrogate families have become quite controversial of late, particularly among those who feel that since God has decreed what sorts of groups we are to live in, that settles the matter, and anyone who chooses to live in a group of any other sort is tantamount to a sinner. "The public continues to receive a steady parade of examples 'proving' that divorced, never-married, homosexual, bisexual, transsexual, communal, and living-together units form the bulk of today's 'families,'" writes Jeane Westin, author of *The Coming Parent Revolution* (1981).

> The most noted "family experts" huddled together for a four-day conference in the late 1970s to answer the question, Who can define "family" in a way everyone would accept? No one pointed out that "family" has always been defined as parents plus children and that family experimenters can jolly well come up with their own concepts rather than asking the traditional family to move over.

Westin asserts, "The continual extension of the concept of family to include every social fad and sexual fancy has resulted in the trivialization of the family."[50]

"If you recall," former senator Roger Jepsen (R-Iowa) told his fellow members of the upper house of Congress in June 1981 when he introduced the then-current version of the Family Protection Act, "after the 1970 White House Conference on Children and Youth, the Forum 14 report redefined the family as a group of individuals in interaction." He continued,

> The American Home Economics Association has determined that the family is a unit of two or more persons who share values and have a commitment to one another over time. Unfortunately, such all-encompassing definitions, which at first glance may appear bland and academically accurate, actually extend the meaning of family to

include anyone and anything from group marriages to homosexual and lesbian couples who want to adopt children.

The question is, why is this "unfortunate"? If the purpose of the family is economic—if, that is, the family is an institution that is entered into by its members in order to improve their overall standard of living and provide themselves with a measure of security during hard times—why isn't any group of individuals who live together for these purposes properly considered a family? If another function of family life is to provide moral and emotional support for family members when they are demoralized, disgraced, or defeated, why isn't any group of individuals who live together and support each other in this way properly considered a family? If still another function of the family is to provide education in living skills for children, why isn't any group of adults and children who live together properly considered a family? If it weren't possible for biologically unrelated individuals to interact satisfactorily as family members, conventional marriage—that is, marriage to nonrelatives—would be impossible, as would adoption. The old adage that you can choose your friends but not your relatives is universally acknowledged to be untrue when it comes to husbands, wives, and adopted children. Why then is it true of parents, grandparents, aunts, uncles, cousins, and siblings?

In fact, people *have* been exercising choice with respect to their family members for hundreds of years, albeit in a more informal manner than the one that typifies legal marriage or adoption. All of us have heard people remark of unusually close friends that "I love him like a brother," or "I love her like a sister," or "She's been like a second mother to me," or "He's like the father (or son or brother) I never had." Many of us have known people who have informally adopted other unrelated adults into their families, shared holidays with them, and named them "honorary" aunts or uncles of their children. Many of us

have friends who are looked upon by all the members of our biological families as loved ones and who are entitled, in our minds,
to the same treatment we would extend to our own brothers or
sisters. We tell these friends to feel free to visit any time, even on
an unannounced basis. We tell them to "make themselves at
home." We lend them our money and our cars and our irreplace-
able treasures—things we make a policy of never lending to
anyone else. We give them keys to our homes, trust them with
our children, turn to them for moral and emotional support. And
we feel able to call upon them in any emergency, just as they feel
able to call upon us. What are these special friends but adopted
family members, people we have adopted without the usual
bureaucratic rigmarole that ordinarily accompanies adoption, but
adopted nonetheless?

Social observers Karen Lindsey and Jonathan Gathorne-Hardy
see this phenomenon of "friends as family" as the wave of the
future. But, as we have seen, it might equally be regarded as the
wave of the past reestablishing itself after a brief apparent absence
during the 1950s. For most of the past two centuries, with the
exception of that brief but crucial period of slightly more than a
decade, the "traditional" family has been merely one of a number
of possible household types, all of which have been common. It
may be useful at this point to repeat the admonition of Levitan and
Belous that "with diminished social pressures to follow any one
pattern"—that is, given the decadent times we live in—"a good
portion of the reported increase in this behavior [unconventional
family types] may represent only the increased willingness of
people to be open about what has always taken place."[51]

But of course such increased openness can only serve to
encourage those who waver between following established social
practice despite the fact that they find it unrewarding and doing
their own things, unconventional though those things may be.
Inevitably, some of the apparent increase in unconventional family
life that we seem to see all around us *is* new, *is* a real increase. It

is the natural tendency of market economies to gradually increase the personal wealth of almost all who participate in their operation. And increased personal wealth means wider personal choice—in the current vernacular, more options. So it is that as per capita income has grown in our country, it has become increasingly possible for more and more people to live in untraditional households. The expanding market for goods and services has led to the establishment of an expanded market for types of families. And the majority of Americans have voted with their feet and their pocketbooks and their hearts for untraditional family lives.

Is there any role for government in all this? If so, what should that role be? There is widespread consensus that there is such a role and that it should be an active one. Letty Cottin Pogrebin speaks for the political left, but no right-wing defender of the family would disagree with her when she writes, "Families might be less sophisticated political activists than the farm or tobacco lobby . . . but who's to claim families are not more entitled to federal supports and subsidies?"[52] No, the only real argument between the liberals and the conservatives when it comes to government family policy is over which kind of family should be singled out for benefit—traditional families or untraditional families. The reactionary right would have government set up incentives so that Americans who opted for traditional family life would be rewarded, often at the expense of those who prefer untraditional family life. The liberal left would have government subsidize untraditional family life, often at the expense of those who prefer traditional family life.

I say a pox on both their houses. To each his or her own. Let government in this country adopt a family policy of laissez-faire. Let each man and woman, and, to the extent that it is feasible, each child, do what he or she wants. They have, all of them, the inestimable advantage of knowing much better than any government bureaucrat exactly *what* they want, and what price they are willing to pay to get it.

16

The Deaths and Lives of Great American Cities

Another consideration, of course, is *where* they'll be able to get it. For some years now, for most American families, living in the United States has meant living in or near cities. The phrase "the crisis of the cities," which most of us have been hearing as long as we've been alive, does *not* mean—*cannot* mean—that we are witnessing and being called to action against some general or overall decline in the importance of the city as an institution, the city per se. More Americans live in cities and metropolitan areas today than ever before in history.

What definitely has been happening over the past half century or so, and particularly during the past three decades, is a steady, unmistakable migration of the American population, not away from cities as such, but away from some cities in favor of others. And, as writer Nicholas Von Hoffman has pointed out, for politicians in the cities that are losing people, "population loss is power loss. In some ways that's what the urban crisis is, the clamor made by the heads of institutions

141

that fear they can't follow the people when they leave for happier climes."

The question is, why are all these people leaving? The most common answers to emerge over the past three decades place the blame on climate, economic changes, and simple old age. *Newsweek* reported in May 1981, for example, that "there has been a massive shift of people and jobs from the Snow Belt cities of the North to the Sun Belt cities of the Southwest. While the older cities struggle to rebuild aging steel mills and auto plants, the newer cities march into the post-industrial world of computers and semi-conductors."

This kind of analysis is plausible enough as far as it goes. People do prefer to live where the climate does not present major obstacles to their comfort, mobility, efficient use of time, and achievement of affluence. And the biggest growth records set by American industry in the past generation have indeed been set by firms in the mainly Sun Belt-based computer and electronics fields.

Still, to blame the urban migration entirely on the weather and the location of most new high-tech industry is to indulge in dangerous oversimplification. Anchorage and Colorado Springs, two of the fastest-growing of the boomtowns of the past two decades, are undeniably in the Snow Belt. And just as undeniably the climate in Phoenix is a forbidding one: those who have visited this rapidly growing city during the summer months might even without fear of argument call it *more* forbidding than the climate of Detroit or Cleveland. Nor is all our new high-tech industry headquartered in California and Texas and Florida. Some of the largest and fastest-growing electronics firms and communications technology companies are headquartered instead in suburban Boston and suburban Chicago. They are in the suburbs rather than in the city proper, it is true; this is a highly significant fact to which I shall return later. But they *are* relatively new high-tech companies, and they are operating and even prospering in the metropolitan areas of Snow Belt cities that, despite such pockets of hope, go right on declining.

Some commentators discuss the differences between the declining cities and the booming cities in terms of age—the older cities are declining and the younger cities are booming. But this explanation, too, is fraught with difficulties. The city of Los Angeles, which is commonly (and, as we shall see, properly) seen as a perfect instance or "ideal type" of the "younger city," celebrated its two-hundredth birthday in 1981. In 1790, at a time when Chicago, Cleveland, and Kansas City were mere Indian villages or frontier trading posts, Los Angeles was only nine people smaller than Louisville, Kentucky, which was founded three years earlier than Los Angeles, in 1778. By 1900 Louisville was twice the size of Los Angeles (204,000 to 102,000); today it is a little less than a tenth the size of Los Angeles. Since 1970 Louisville has lost approximately 25 percent of its population; the population of Los Angeles has grown nearly 25 percent in the same period. Louisville is not an older city than Los Angeles. They are almost exact contemporaries. But one of them grew more rapidly and then declined, while the other has continued to grow.

Nor is this an isolated phenomenon. San Antonio, Texas, and Akron, Ohio, were also founded at about the same time, circa 1825. San Antonio has always been the larger of the two, but as time has gone by, the gap has widened noticeably. In 1900 San Antonio had a population of 53,000 to Akron's 42,000, which means the Texas city was about 25 percent larger than its Ohio sister. By 1950 San Antonio was the twenty-fifth largest American city, with a population of 400,000, while Akron was the thirty-ninth largest, with 275,000 people. Today San Antonio is our ninth largest, with nearly a million residents, while Akron has slipped to seventy-fifth, with only 220,000. San Antonio is now more than 400 percent larger than Akron.

Houston and Milwaukee are another instructive pair. Milwaukee is the younger of the two by one year, having been founded in 1837 to Houston's 1836. At first Milwaukee grew much more rapidly: in 1850 the Wisconsin city was already nearly ten times the size of its Texas cousin. But by 1960, when Milwaukee's population reached its all-time high of nearly 750,000, Houston's had grown to 940,000. Today Houston is at 1.7 million and still growing, while Milwaukee has fallen back to 617,000—after a nearly 15 percent drop in population since 1970. Houston is also an older city than Atlanta (founded in 1847), but it is Atlanta that is declining. The population of Georgia's biggest city has fallen by nearly 20 percent since 1970, while Houston's population has grown by more than 30 percent.

But if weather and economic trends and old age aren't the answer, what is? Why *are* so many of our cities declining? The true answer has been a matter of public record at least since the early years of Jimmy Carter's presidency—it was printed in the controversial final report of Carter's Commission for a National Agenda for the Eighties: "Contrary to conventional wisdom," the report stated, "cities are not permanent; their strength is related to their ability to reflect change rather than to fend it off." And those American cities which are now in decline have, by and large, brought their decline on themselves by trying to fend off one of the most powerful and comprehensive forces for change to appear in human civilization for centuries—the advent of the automobile.

Barely a hundred years ago, there was no such thing as an automobile; today it is all around us, and there is no escaping its all-pervasive influence on American society. Without it, more than 88 percent of our workforce would have to find some other way of getting to work—if they still had jobs to go to. One out of every six jobs in this country owes its existence to the automotive industry. More than 90 percent of all personal transportation in this country is by private car. More than 80 percent of all commercial transportation is by truck. Nearly 90 percent of all American adults drive. At least 130 million Americans own their own cars. Cars have made insurance, tourism, rubber, and petroleum into giant industries and have created other industries where none had existed before: the motel business, the service station business, the car wash and car repair and rent-a-car and parking businesses. Cars have given us drive-in movies, drive-in restaurants, and drive-in convenience stores, to say nothing of drive-through banks, drive-through photo developers, and drive-through fast-food joints.

Moreover, from *The Great Gatsby* to *The Grapes of Wrath* to *On the Road* and *Play It as It Lays*; from *Zen and the Art of Motorcycle Maintenance* to *Easy Rider*; from *Tobacco Road* to *Thunder Road* to *Rebel Without a Cause*; and from "In My Merry Oldsmobile" to "Route 66" to "Wake Up, Little Susie" to "Little Deuce Coupe" and the scores of trucker ballads ground out annually by our country music industry, the automobile has become one of the central symbols of our national folklore and a staple image in American literature, film, and popular song. It has become literally one of the cornerstones of American culture, and for a reason so obvious that it needs periodic restatement to prevent its being entirely forgotten: our culture draws both its distinctive national character and its remarkable fecundity and durability from a fundamental and unshakable commitment to exactly the sort of self-reliant individualism and personal freedom that have found their most advanced technological expression to date in the development of the automobile.

The car, writes John Rae in his classic, indispensable study, *The Road and the Car in American Life* (1971), "offers individual, personal, flexible mobility, as nothing before it has ever done, and as nothing else now available can do."[53] The car, writes David Laird in a recent essay on the automobile in American fiction, offers "enclosure, security, individual autonomy and control, freedom to do as one pleases."[54] The problem with most "reflections on the impact of the automobile," writes economist Robert A. Heilbroner, is that they

> still fail to do justice to its quintessential contribution to our lives. This is its gift of mobility itself . . . as a direct enhancement of life, as an enlargement of life's boundaries and opportunities. This is so enormous, so radical a transformation that its effect can no longer be measured or appreciated by mere figures. It is nothing less than the unshackling of the age-old bonds of locality; it is the grant of geographic choice and economic freedom on a hitherto unimagined scale.[55]

If A. J. Liebling was right in his contention that freedom of the press belongs to the man who owns one, then it would seem indisputable that freedom of movement belongs to the man who has some means of getting about—and only to the extent of that means' efficiency and flexibility—which is why, for the person who owns (or leases or rents) one, the automobile is truly the machine of freedom.

The truth of this point is acknowledged even by the most hysterical of the automobile's opponents and detractors—even by A. Q. Mowbray, author of *Road to Ruin* (1969), who believes that unless we are prepared "to limit by fiat the manufacture of cars and trucks; to coerce car owners by tax or otherwise to use public transportation; to close state and city borders to visitors approaching by car; to tear up rather than to build freeways, garages, bridges, and tunnels," we will shortly reach a time when "the environment will have become utterly hostile to human life."[56] Even Mowbray, has noticed that auto ownership

> confers many blessings: unparalleled freedom of action, opportunities for travel and home location, and simply the pleasures of tooling around aimlessly. The possibilities for movement seem infinite, and all with a degree of independence and privacy never before achieved. . . . The automobile gives its owner multiple choices in spades—he goes where he wants to go, when he wants to go, and stops when *he* is ready, and not before.[57]

Automotive historians generally agree that it was the desire for exactly such independence, autonomy, and control over one's personal movement that made Americans such enthusiastic buyers of cars from the very first moment of their availability in the American marketplace. Those who lived on farms or in rural towns, for example, welcomed the freedom to *really* take their business elsewhere if they couldn't find what they wanted in the mail-order catalogs and the few small stores of limited inventory that they had nearby. They welcomed the freedom to live in the country without having to worry that their distance from centers of medical treatment might someday lead to the death of one of their loved ones. They also welcomed the freedom to use more of their time satisfying their own personal desires—a freedom they were given not only by the Model T, which shortened the span of hours they had periodically to spend on trips into town, but also by the Fordson tractor, introduced by Ford shortly after the Model T, which dramatically shortened the time they had to spend in the fields.

By 1926, according to Harvard researcher Joseph Interrante, 89 percent of the tenants and 93 percent of the farmers in the prototypical farm state of Iowa owned automobiles. And after the advent of the car, writes Michael Berger in his book *The Devil Wagon in God's Country* (1979),

> everything was more complex. No longer did one choose friends, leisure activities, or the family doctor merely on the basis of proximity. The new associations included people from geographically separate units, and interest rather than location became the primary tie among them. As John H. Kolb and Edmund deS. Brunner concluded in 1935, "rural society is becoming less dependent upon locality and organic relationships and is freer to employ voluntary and contractual forms." Time ceased to be the barrier it had once been.[58]

For those who lived in the cities, the story was much the same. Before the car, city dwellers found it necessary to live within easy walking distance of their jobs and the stores where they shopped. Never mind that the housing immediately adjacent to the factories where most of them worked was almost always crowded, dirty, and noisy. Never mind that the prices were high in the small neighborhood shops where they were forced by circumstances to do all their business. Never mind that such shops offered only a limited selection of merchandise at their high prices. They city dweller in nineteenth-century America lived in the land of Hobson's Choice: he could take whatever his neighborhood happened to offer or nothing at all.

This situation was improved somewhat during the last three decades of the last century by the fairly extensive development of fixed-rail urban transit, at first in the form of horse-drawn streetcars and trolleys and then in the form of electric or steam-driven streetcars, trolleys, and commuter trains. Urban rail transit markedly increased the options available to city dwellers, but only within certain very narrow limits. You had to want to go where the rails led; if you had another destination in mind, the streetcars, trolleys, and trains couldn't help you. You had to be willing to go when the transit company (commonly a city-granted monopoly) was ready to take you. And you had to put up with a lot: "Travelers on urban fixed-rail trolleys," writes Mark H. Rose in *Interstate: Express Highway Politics, 1941–1956* (1979),

> all faced encounters with pickpockets, drunks, thugs, and the obnoxious. Streetcars themselves were dreadfully over-crowded. Passengers were "packed like sardines in a box, with perspiration for oil" and were forced to "hang on by the straps, like smoked hams in a corner grocery."[59]

"With conditions like these prevailing in our mass transit systems," writes A. Q. Mowbray, "we need not wonder why transit riders reacted to the automobile like a starving man in a supermarket. Here was comfort, convenience, privacy, independence."[60] Here also was a way out of the city. Whether one wanted to get out for a few hours or a couple of days on an outing in the newly accessible countryside or to get out for good, abandoning the city for life in the suburbs where one could afford a house instead of an apartment and relax on one's own land instead of on some corner of a crowded public park—one could do it if one had a car. And one could leave the city in any direction one liked. It no longer mattered where the rails led.

The rest, as they say, is history. Beginning around the time of World War I, rising to a peak in the late 1920s, falling off somewhat during the Depression and World War II years, then rising again over the next quarter-century to hitherto undreamed-of levels, people got out of the cities. As early as 1908 the advertising profession had seen the beginnings of this trend. In *The Road and the Car in American Life,* John Rae quotes an auto ad of that year: "The Sears is the car for the business man who has tired of home life in a congested neighborhood and yearns for a cottage in the suburb for his family."[61]

"The outward trend of population in American cities," Rae comments,

> was clearly visible in the 1920s. Figures for eighty-five metropolitan districts (which would now be termed SMSAs) show a growth pattern in which the rate of increase for outlying territory was twice as great as in the central cities. At that time the suburban population was 30.0 percent of the metropolitan total, although in eleven of these districts the population outside the central cities was already greater than that inside. In addition, there was evidence of a tendency for large cities to lose population in their inner zones.[62]

Half a century later, this tendency had become even more pronounced. Between 1950 and 1970, according to Landon Y. Jones in *Great Expectations: America and the Baby Boom Generation,* "the population of the suburbs doubled from 36 million to 72 million. No less than 83 percent of the total population growth in the United States during the 1950s was in the suburbs, which were growing fifteen times faster than any other segment of the country."[63]

And by 1980, the authors of the final report of the President's Commission for a National Agenda for the Eighties could write that

> although more than 70 percent of the U.S. population still lives in metropolitan areas, migration to the suburbs continues, and since 1970, there has been a reversal of the traditional movement in the United States toward the cities. People are now moving away from the cities entirely—to rural areas and small towns.

Of course, as we have seen, it can be misleading to say that people are leaving "the cities," because in fact they are leaving some cities and moving into others. And much of the current movement away from cities to small towns and rural areas will doubtless be seen retrospectively to have been movement to the suburbs. Thirty years ago, a family that moved from Houston to La Porte, Texas, would have been leaving a city and relocating in a small town surrounded by farmland. Today a family moving from Houston to La Porte would simply be making a move to the suburbs, and not even to one of the farthest-flung of Houston's suburbs, which now continue some miles past La Porte into nearby Galveston County. Eighty years ago, Hollywood was a small town at the foot of the mountains north of Los Angeles, and was separated from the city by miles of open fields. Today Hollywood is generally regarded as part of the inner city of Los Angeles. Times change.

And they change for business as well as for families. Since World War II, American industry has also been relocating in the suburbs—or, in the case of heavy industries, in the country beyond the suburbs. John Rae reports that

> in an eight-year period (1947 to 1954) the number of industrial plants in Chicago's suburbs doubled; during the same eight years Detroit had a 47 percent increase in central city manufacturing establishments but a 220 percent rise in the suburbs. At longer range and on a broader scale, before the Second World War nine out of ten new factories were built in metropolitan areas; by the mid-1950s new

construction was about even divided between urban and country districts; subsequently the proportion of new factories located outside metropolitan regions has risen to 80 percent—a striking measure of the extent of industrial dispersal.[64]

This passage was written in 1970. Since then the trend has continued. "Businesses have relocated in suburbia at a rate equal to that of families," William Severini Kowinski wrote in the *New York Times Magazine* early in 1980.

New York City's share of metropolitan area employment dropped from 65 percent in 1953 to 52 percent in 1976. Thomas Muller, principal research associate of the Urban Institute, cites this loss of private employment as a major factor in New York City's fiscal crisis. The same could be said of Chicago, Boston and other cities.[65]

And in the '90s, think of the phenomenal growth of the computer and computer-related industries in California's San Francisco Bay Area. This growth has been a principal factor in making the region one of the most dynamic and populous in the nation. But where has the growth taken place? Not in San Francisco, the region's urban center, but in "Silicon Valley," a suburban and still partly rural area around fifty miles south of what Bay Area residents refer to as "The City."

Why have businesses been leaving these cities? In the case of retail businesses, the answer is obvious enough: in pursuit of their departing customers. But in the case of manufacturing industry, the answer is more complex. "First," writes John Rae,

is the rapid development of industrial technologies stressing continuous flow of materials and automatic controls, which may require production processes involving straight-line movements of considerable length. In addition, modern methods of handling materials with mechanized equipment, such as conveyors and fork-lift trucks, work best in one-story structures. These factors in combination demand space and therefore encourage location where the cost of land is comparatively low, a condition more likely to be met in outlying than in central city areas.[66]

Of course, as Rae points out,

> this incentive to disperse must be balanced against other considera-
> tions. The factory has to have a site permitting ready movement of
> goods in and out and accessible to the work force. In the past these
> factors limited locational choices, since the places where land was
> plentiful and cheap were likely to have inadequate transportation and
> to have too few people within practical traveling distance. The motor
> vehicle and the highway greatly expanded the options. The pas-
> senger car solves much of the problem of personnel and is a major
> locational factor in its own right, allowing a plant to be in open
> country and draw its labor supply from as far as thirty to forty miles.
> Parking facilities, in fact, may require more land than the plant itself,
> another incentive to seek open space.[67]

So it was that the advent of the car influenced businesses to move out of the central city. But another automobile called the truck was an even greater influence. In the late nineteenth century, the transportation of people, both within cities and between cities, was accomplished primarily by fixed-rail systems. The transportation of *goods,* on the other hand, was accomplished by rail only when the goods were traveling from one city to another. When they were traveling *within* cities, or to towns too small or too recently established to be served by rail lines, they went by horse and wagon. The introduction of the truck in the early 1900s changed all this. Trucks proved to be a much faster method of getting goods to their destinations, and time was money then just as it is today. So trucks quickly replaced horse-drawn wagons within cities and began gradually to supplant the railroads as intercity carriers as well. As new towns and cities sprang up— and as certain older ones gradually grew larger—it was discovered that these new population centers could be served by truck much more cheaply than by train, if only because establishing train service required immense capital outlays for the construction of new tracks, while trucks were able to use the roads that were already there.

Unfortunately, the era of the truck created problems for the very manufacturers who were trying to save money by converting to truck transport—the problem of congestion, for example, which filled the narrow streets around their inner-city factories with nightmares of tangled vehicles and threatened to create delays that would eat up the savings they had hoped for by switching to trucks in the first place. There was no question of constructing off-street parking areas and loading docks for the trucks: the space wasn't available, or if it was the price was prohibitive. On the other hand, if the factory were to move to the country outside the city, it could provide plenty of space for plenty of trucks at relatively low cost. And although moving out of town would put the factory at a distance from rail terminals, that was no longer as big a problem as it once had been. After all, the owners could merely cease relying on the railroads altogether and use trucks for all their transportation requirements. Thus began the exodus of industry from most of the old central cities.

And thus it is that today we live in a country in which the typical American is a suburbanite, in which a majority of our fellow citizens live in suburbs rather than in central cities or rural areas, in which the lion's share of the nation's business is now out in the suburbs, and in which virtually the only cities not suffering from steady and apparently irreversible decline are those which have adapted to the automobile by becoming more suburban—that is, less dense, more decentralized and auto-accessible—in character. When everybody drives his or her own vehicle, there's more traffic and more of a parking problem and really very little question—in any city of more than a million people, at least—of being able to build any single central business district that could possibly be at once compact enough to be genuinely centralized, generous enough in the wideness of its thoroughfares to keep traffic flowing smoothly, and lavish enough in its parking facilities to accommodate all the cars of all its workers and shoppers and players all at once. The car and the old centralized city are fundamentally incompatible.

The city of the automotive age, on the other hand, is *decen-*
tralized. It has not one central business district but several. In Los
Angeles, for example, the largest and best known of our decentralized cities, there is Downtown, which houses the city's governmental buildings, its convention center, its music center, and
its garment district; Hollywood, which provides a home for one
of the city's largest medical centers, along with a major proportion of its bookstores, record shops, and movie theaters, a generous selection of its best restaurants, and, of course, the radio,
TV, and film industries that have made Los Angeles the international center that it is today; and Century City, the "downtown"
of the airport area that also, in effect, absorbs the high-rise office
towers and luxury hotels that spill over from Downtown and the
entertainment that spills over from Hollywood. There are also
the extensively developed central downtown sections of four
important "close-in" suburban cities—Beverly Hills (which is so
close-in that it has long been completely surrounded by Los
Angeles), Glendale, Pasadena, and Long Beach. And there are
the "downtowns" that have gradually developed over the past
quarter-century in Westwood (adjacent to UCLA) and Van Nuys
(near three large commuter schools—Valley College, Pierce College, and California State University at Northridge). Finally,
there is the Wilshire Corridor, the roughly seven-mile-long strip
of continuous commercial and retail development along Wilshire
Boulevard between Downtown and Beverly Hills.

Angelenos in search of employment, shopping, or entertainment of the sort traditionally found in central business districts
are likely to be able to find what they want in any one of these
ten central business districts and so will usually tend to visit the
ones closest to their homes. But should they need to travel to one
of the others, they will find it easy to get there by car—either via
freeway or via wide, fast-moving "surface streets" like the city's
major, six-lane east-west thoroughfare, Olympic Boulevard—
and easy to park once they have arrived. They may travel more

miles in the course of their shopping trips than their counterparts in centralized cities, but they may very likely invest less *time* in the project. And, as John Rae has noted, "the essential element of transportation for a modern metropolis" is the realization that "the time required to complete a journey is more important than the distance traveled."[68]

The automobile is usually so much faster than any form of surface public transit that it makes distance within an urban area virtually irrelevant—whether you're an individual or a business. Rae reported in 1971 that "companies that relocated along the Santa Ana Freeway in Southern California" shortly after that freeway was opened in the early 1960s quickly "found that the travel time to central Los Angeles was less than from their former intown sites."[69] Even in rush-hour traffic in the heart of the central business district, the automobile is usually faster than its alternatives. Wilfred Owen reported in a Brookings Institution study in 1966—long before downtown congestion had become what it is today—that cars averaged 14 miles per hour in such circumstances in Washington, while transit vehicles that also operated on the surface averaged only 8 miles per hour. In Philadelphia, the situation was comparable: cars averaged 8.3 miles per hour in downtown rush-hour traffic, while surface mass-transit vehicles were able to manage only 5.6 miles per hour. Nor is the reason for this discrepancy far to seek: the private passenger car, being much smaller and more maneuverable than a bus or streetcar, is much better equipped to make quick lane changes and take advantage of sudden breaks in traffic flow; moreover, unlike buses and streetcars, a private passenger car need not stop to disgorge and pick up passengers at every block.

Even under the worst of conditions, the automobile is usually a more efficient means of transportation—in addition to offering a degree of individual autonomy, privacy, and personal choice in transit that could not possibly be delivered by any alternative now known to human science. Is it any wonder that Americans have opted for it so overwhelmingly? The automobile is the machine of freedom, and the decentralized or polycentric city it has brought into being is better equipped than any city of any other known type to accommodate all at once all the many disparate choices, decisions, and actions of millions of individuals, each of whom has the power to move himself at will to any urban or suburban destination of his choice. The decentralized city is the best framework yet developed for the spontaneous order of a free market in mobility, perhaps because the decentralized city is itself the product of such spontaneous order, of the predominantly free interaction of past market forces. As the President's Commission for a National Agenda for the Eighties argued:

> Federal urban policy efforts should not necessarily be used to discourage the deconcentration and dispersal of industry and households from central locations. Each emerging deconcentration trend is nothing more than an aggregate of countless choices by and actions of individuals, families, and firms influenced by social, cultural, and economic considerations; our public policy tools are least useful when they attempt to alter in a predictable way what the individual household or firm will do.

It was neatly symbolic of the official view of the automobile and urban decentralization that President Carter publicly rejected his commission's findings on the crisis of the cities literally as soon as they were presented to him. For from the very beginning, ever since the days when police in a number of American towns were legally empowered to keep cars outside the town limits by shooting at their tires and by stretching ropes or chains across local roads to block their progress, public policy on every level of American government has almost always been virulently anticar and procentralization.

This view of our recent transit history is, of course, violently at variance with the current conventional wisdom on the subject. But then the conventional wisdom on almost every subject is almost invariably wrong. In this case the conventional wisdom contends that the automobile has come to dominate our transportation horizon because it has been the beneficiary of massive government subsidies, principally in the form of federal and state freeway and superhighway programs and government-funded construction of parking facilities in central business districts. These roads and garages, it is argued, induced people to abandon public transit and buy cars. Otherwise, the argument goes, they might not have done so, or they might have done so in smaller numbers.

Such an argument requires for its success either an extreme credulity or a profound ignorance of the history of urban transit on the part of those it is intended to convince—though its partisans have also profited to some extent from the Big Lie technique first described in the abstract by Adolf Hitler: tell a preposterous falsehood often enough, loudly enough, and with enough self-assurance, and everyone will soon come to believe it. It is true, of course, that our roads are government-built. But, by and large, they always have been in this country. Was government supposed to stop building them after the invention of the automobile in order to discourage use of the new invention?

It is also true that one is more likely to buy a car if there is a road to drive it on than if there isn't. But it is absurd to try to pretend that there were no roads in the pre-automotive era. On the contrary, as John Rae points out,

> analysis of the data reveals that motor vehicle transportation actually requires *less* street space than most cities had in the pre-automobile era, *even including the substantial area taken by freeways.* The reason is that when the fast-moving through traffic is put on built-for-the-purpose arterial roads, then the amount of ordinary street space needed for strictly local movements and for access to property drops sharply.[70] (Emphasis added)

An urban freeway system, he argues, can carry upwards of 50 percent of all urban traffic on only 2 to 3 percent of the land. Moreover, he writes,

what applies to city streets applies equally to the entire national
highway network; most of the roads would have to be there even if
the motor vehicle did not exist. They would be different in quality,
but the same mileage of roads at the very least would be needed for
local transport.[71]

For maximum efficiency of performance and maximum
comfort of passengers, automobiles do require better quality
roads than would otherwise be necessary. But they do *not* require
better roads in order to function at all. Automobiles caught on so
quickly in the early years of this century, long before there were
any government-built freeways to tempt people to buy them,
precisely because they made for an enormous improvement in
the quality and efficiency of transportation *despite the fact that
they had to travel over mostly inadequate roads.* Freeways and
widened, resurfaced urban streets were a reaction to the coming
of the car, not a cause of it.

And when the time came to make these improvements in our
roads, the owners of automobiles paid for it through gasoline
taxes, tire taxes, and other approximations of user fees. "One of
the great changes that automotive transportation has brought
about, at least in the United States," John Rae wrote nearly three
decades ago, "is that user taxes make the highway system self-
supporting."[72] Unfortunately, this is no longer true, though it
would be if the trucking industry didn't use its political muscle
to avoid paying its fair share—that is to say, the lion's share—of
the cost of road maintenance. It is trucks and buses that create the
need for major road maintenance in the first place. The passage
of ordinary passenger cars has almost no effect on the surface of
a modern road.

Still, there are today freeway links that have been built and
maintained with public funds, that carry massive amounts of
daily traffic, including trucks and buses, and that nevertheless are
more than self-supporting through user fees. In the San Francisco
Bay Area, for example, the two busiest toll bridges, the Golden

Gate Bridge and the San Francisco-Oakland Bay Bridge, have long since paid off the entire cost of their construction, including interest on the amounts borrowed for the projects, and continue to produce revenues so far in excess of what is needed to keep them in good repair that they can also pick up the staggering losses posted each year by the AC Transit bus and Golden Gate Transit bus and ferry companies. *This* is the typical pattern of public policy toward the automobile and the decentralized, freeway-based city: not subsidies for automotive transport, but levies of taxes against automobiles and their drivers in order to subsidize mass-transit boondoggles that have never at any time in the past half-century been able even to meet their own costs of operation, much less earn a profit.

It is possible to cite at least one recent example of an urban freeway being built by private businessmen operating without the power of eminent domain and without government money— the Hardy Toll Road which operates on the crowded north side of Houston. And it is easy to cite cases of privately built parking facilities that earn respectable profits. But where is there a case today of a privately owned and privately capitalized subway or streetcar system? The question answers itself. Such systems are everywhere publicly funded, and they everywhere lose money— even in cities like New York, where almost everyone uses them.

Outside New York, in fact—and Boston and Philadelphia and Washington and Chicago and San Francisco—scarcely anybody uses them. More than 88 percent of us go to work every day by car, either our own or someone else's. Another 3 percent of us walk to work. Only about 5 percent of us take mass transit. Almost as many people walk as take mass transit. Walking, like driving, enables us to go where we want when we want by the route we want and in the company we want, without having to stop unless we want. Autonomy. Freedom of choice. Self-reliant individualism. Decadence.

When will we acknowledge at last that these are the values

that have built the car culture and crippled the old centralized city? When will we acknowledge that most Americans, given their druthers, want personal freedom, personal privacy, a little space between themselves and their neighbors, a lot of independence from centralized systems, and an opportunity to live in relatively homogeneous communities where most of the people and their houses and their lifestyles are pretty similar? When will we acknowledge that the modern, decentralized city that looks like a cluster of suburbs with no one center is the kind of city most Americans prefer? When will we acknowledge that for cities in the automotive age, it is sprawl or die—and that this is the reason Los Angeles, Houston, San Antonio, San Diego, and Phoenix are booming while New York, Chicago, and Atlanta are in decline? And when will we stop fighting it? When will we stop squandering our resources in a futile attempt to stop change, fight the passage of time, and preserve a mode of living that, outside a few still traditional urban centers with a population deeply devoted to the ways of the past, has been trying for decades to lie down and die quietly, and with dignity?

17

The Crisis of Civility

Still, it might be argued, even if we acknowledge that what decadence has done to our families and our cities is, generally, for the best; even if we acknowledge that decadence has served well even those of a more traditionalist stripe (by making it easier than ever to go off and live amongst others of the same stripe, away from the dizzying diversity that has come to typify the cultural mainstream); even then, it must also be acknowledged—mustn't it?—that decadence has coarsened our society, undermined the civility that once underlay it, rendered it rude and increasingly unpleasant to navigate.

Consider, for example, the sort of behavior that has come in recent years to be described as "sexual harassment." The term *sexual harassment* seems to have entered the English language sometime during the late 1960s or early 1970s, apparently in the United States. By 1975, it had been officially recognized in U.S. federal courts—the first courts anywhere in the world to extend such official recognition—as a prohibited form of sexual discrimination.

But it wasn't until fifteen or sixteen years later, at the beginning of the 1990s, that "sexual harassment" made the national news in a big way and became a household term all over the United States. It wasn't until the dawn of the 1990s that most people in this country had any idea what "sexual harassment" was.

Then came the confirmation hearings before the Senate Judiciary Committee in the case of Clarence Thomas, who had been nominated to fill a vacancy on the U.S. Supreme Court by President George Bush. Thomas was a controversial nominee from the beginning. He was a black conservative, which meant that both liberals and most prominent black Americans attacked him vociferously. But then an attractive, articulate, intelligent, black woman law professor named Anita Hill came forward. She had worked under Thomas's supervision some years before, and she now accused Thomas of having sexually harassed her at the time. *Now* the nomination became *really* controversial. For weeks during 1991, you couldn't open a newspaper or turn on a television news or public affairs program without encountering Thomas's celebrated witticisms about pubic hairs on Coca-Cola cans and a male organ called "Long Dong Silver."

Ultimately, Thomas was confirmed and took his seat on the Supreme Court; Anita Hill returned to Oklahoma to teach. But the issue they had elevated to national attention did not retire from the spotlight as they did. Far from it.

Only about a year later, another "sexual harassment" scandal rocked the nation's capitol—this one involving Republican Senator Bob Packwood of Oregon. Packwood had been a fixture in the Senate for a quarter-century; he had first been sent there by his fellow Oregonians in 1968, in the same election that put Richard Nixon in the White House. It is agreed by virtually everyone on every side of the controversy that began swirling around him in 1992 that during his twenty-four years in the Senate, Packwood not only consistently and effectively championed the causes of women's rights groups, but also set an exemplary Senate record in hiring a majority of women for his own staff, long before the idea of "sex discrimination" had attained any currency at all, and in helping to advance the careers of his female aides on merit. Now Packwood was accused of having made unwelcome sexual advances to seventeen women during those years. It took nearly three more years, but in the end, these charges—along with some others, including charges of improperly using his office to obtain employment for friends and family—brought Packwood down; he resigned from the Senate in September 1995, knowing that if he remained much longer he was likely to be expelled by his colleagues.

As I say, all this got a great deal of airtime and a great deal of ink back in the early '90s, not only for coverage of the Packwood case, but also for commentary on it. Packwood had both his defenders and his detractors. His defenders pointed out that, on Capitol Hill, where sexual harassment was concerned, "everybody was doing it"; Packwood was only being singled out for unwarranted abuse. After all, a *Washington Post* poll showed that 11 percent of all female congressional staffers said they had been sexually harassed by at least one congressman during their careers. The fact that everyone is doing it, Packwood's detractors replied, does *not* make it right.

Packwood had his advocates and his critics even among women. On the one hand there was Dr. Ruth Westheimer. Setting aside the charges that Packwood had illegally used his office to advance the interests of friends and family, Dr. Ruth told the *Los Angeles Times* in September, the senator's only real transgression had been

> that he couldn't distinguish those women who appreciated his advances from those who did not. When some women literally throw themselves at you, it's easy to get confused and think that every woman is eager for your attentions. Yes, he was wrong for being overly aggressive, but could any of us who might be put in his place guarantee that we wouldn't make the same mistake?[73]

Then, on the other hand, there was *San Francisco Chronicle* columnist Debra J. Saunders. "[P]oor Packwood would have you blame his environment," she wrote in December.

> He works with an army of swells who can't pat themselves on the back enough in recognition of all the fine things they've done with other people's money. Why what woman in her right mind, they must wonder in their shallow hearts, would not be flattered by their manly advances?[74]

Whatever you may have thought of Bob Packwood back in the early '90s, however, if you thought anything about him at all, it was hard to get away from sexual harassment; even if you systematically ignored coverage of the Packwood case, sexual harassment came at you from all directions—it was everywhere.

It was on the campus of the University of Michigan, for example. There in Ann Arbor, in October 1992, about a month before the accusations against Senator Packwood were first aired, a student named Shawn Brown, a sophomore, wrote the following paragraph in a seven-page paper on opinion polls for an introductory political science course.

> Another problem with sampling polls is that some people desire their privacy and don't want to be bothered by a pollster. Let's say Dave Stud is entertaining three beautiful ladies in his penthouse when the phone rings. A pollster on the other end wants to know if we should eliminate the capital-gains tax. Now, Dave is a knowledgeable businessperson who cares a lot about this issue. But since Dave is "tied up" at the moment, he tells the pollster to "bother" someone else. Now, this is perhaps a ludicrous example, but there is simply a segment of the population who wish to be left alone.[75]

When Shawn Brown got his paper back, he found a paragraph written in red in the margin next to his paragraph. The red paragraph was written by Debbie Meizlish, a graduate student and teaching assistant in the Political Science Department. Her paragraph read:

You are right. This is ludicrous & inappropriate & OFFENSIVE. This is completely inappropriate for a serious political science paper. It completely violates the standard of non-sexist writing. Professor Rosenstone has encouraged me to interpret this comment as an example of sexual harassment and to take the appropriate formal steps. I have chosen not to do so in this instance. However, any future comments, in a paper, in a class, or in any dealings me, will be interpreted as sexual harassment and formal steps *will be* taken. Professor Rosenstone is aware of these comments—& is prepared to intervene. You are forewarned![76]

Shawn dropped the course. When the paper, with Debbie's comments, was called to the attention of the chair of the Political Science Department, that eminent professor—unnamed in the news accounts I have seen of this matter—stated his or her support for the offended teaching assistant's action. In those days— as in ours, a few short years later—extremism in the attempt to wipe out sexual harassment was no vice.

And especially not when sexual harassment was so rampant on campus! In March 1993, 54 percent of girls at Berkeley High, in one of the nation's hotbeds of liberalism, progressivism, and political correctness, reported that they had been sexually harassed. Two months later, in June, a nationwide study by the American Association of University Women concluded that 81 percent of girls in grades K through twelve had suffered some amount of sexual harassment.

Individual cases also made headlines. There was the publicized case of eight-year-old Cheltzie Hentz of suburban Minneapolis, who won a court case against her school district in April 1993 after proving she had been sexually harassed by grade-school boys on the school bus. There was the case of Santa Rosa Junior College in Northern California's celebrated "Wine Country," which, according to published reports in 1994, agreed to pay two female students $15,000 each to settle a pending sexual harassment lawsuit the women had filed when they discovered that derogatory sexual remarks about them had been posted on a Men Only computer bulletin board operated by the college. Only a few months earlier, in December 1993, the California Fair Employment and Housing Commission had ruled that colleges and universities could be held legally responsible for sexual harassment that occurred on campus.

A month before that, in November 1993, the U.S. Supreme Court had jumped with both feet into the sexual harassment sweepstakes, issuing an even more sweeping ruling. The high court had agreed to hear an appeal of a case originally filed by Teresa Harris of Nashville, Tennessee. Harris had been the manager of a forklift company there, but had quit her job some years earlier after she felt she could no longer tolerate her boss's boorish behavior. Among other things, he had called her a "dumb-ass woman" in the presence of other employees, asked her to fetch coins from his front pockets, and suggested she come with him to a nearby Holiday Inn to negotiate a raise she had requested. Instead, she sued on grounds of sexual harassment. The lower courts ruled against her because Harris was unable to show that she had been damaged. But the U.S. Supreme Court reversed those rulings. The Supreme Court found that a plaintiff does not have to show that she has suffered what Justice Sandra Day O'Connor called "tangible effects" from sexual harassment, but only that the behavior which was directed at her would *offend* what Justice O'Connor described as a "reasonable person."

And with that, you might say, the cat was out of the bag. Just in case anyone back in the early '90s had been laboring under the delusion that "sexual harassment" was something new, Justice O'Connor was setting that delusional person straight. In fact "sexual harassment" was merely a new name for something very old indeed. As Miss Manners put it in a column that ran in the *San Francisco Chronicle* not long after the Supreme Court's ruling, "Most of what are passing as new social sins are not new at all, but violations of rules that have always been on the etiquette books."

"Sexual harassment," she continued,

is merely a new name for ungentlemanly (or unladylike) behavior that is also unprofessional behavior—two grievous violations of etiquette. No, there never was a time when ladies were flattered to have their attractiveness assessed, much less probed, on the job. There was just a time when they were too afraid of losing their jobs to mention it.

But could this be true? Between 1989 and 1994, the number of federal filings by individuals suing companies for sexual harassment more than doubled. In the first two years after the Anita Hill–Clarence Thomas imbroglio, the number of on-the-job sexual-harassment complaints filed with the Equal Employment Opportunity Commission grew by more than 50 percent. According to the International Labor Organization, by the beginning of 1993, sexual harassment was causing 6 to 8 percent of working women in twenty-three industrialized countries to change their jobs, and 15 to 30 percent were experiencing serious problems such as unwanted touching, offensive sexual commentary, and unwelcome requests for sexual intercourse. Were all these millions of women complaining about nothing more than bad manners?

So it would seem. Consider the testimony of Jean Lang, the Minnesota lawyer who, in 1993, won the first sexual-harassment lawsuit ever tried as a class-action suit. "If you had to have a setup for a first case, this one was perfect," Lang told a *San Francisco Chronicle* reporter early in 1994, "Men were grabbing women's crotches, drawing graffiti showing a map of women's hot spots and telling women that if they wanted to work there, they would have to stand up and piss like men."[77]

The company Lang successfully sued already had an official company policy in place against sexual harassment. Many American companies adopted such policies in the late 1970s and early 1980s after a 1976 federal court decision in effect made sexual harassment illegal. But, as Jean Lang explains when she describes the need for lawsuits of the type she successfully fielded through the courts, such policies are insufficient: "If you think people are suddenly going to act nice to each other just because a company has a policy of equality, you're kidding yourself," she told the *San Francisco Chronicle.* "Too many people just don't behave like they ought to."

Think about that wording for a minute. "If you think people are suddenly going to *act nice* to each other just because a company has a policy of equality, you're kidding yourself. . . . Too many people just don't behave like they ought to."

May I paraphrase? People ought to be nice. If they aren't, they should be prosecuted or sued. They should be taken to court for not being nice.

Think about the implications of that. Susan L. Webb of Seattle is the author of *Shockwaves: The Global Impact of Sexual Harassment,* and a consultant who hires herself out to corporations eager to protect themselves from the legal and financial consequences of not taking the idea of "sexual harassment" with sufficient seriousness. She says: "There isn't always a clear line, so each sexual-harassment case has to be considered in its own context. The standard the courts use is whether a 'reasonable person' would consider the behavior or environment abusive or hostile."[78]

"Since most targets of sexual harassment are women," comment Dianne Hales and Dr. Robert Hales in a 1994 article in *Parade* magazine,

> that usually translates into what a reasonable woman would think, which may be quite different from a man's view. The psychologist Barbara Gutek once asked 1200 men and women how they would view a sexual proposition in the workplace. About 67 percent of the men said they'd find it flattering, while 63 percent of the women said they'd be insulted.[79]

Remember the girls at Berkeley High? Six months or so after they reported the serious problems they were having with sexual harassment on campus, the Berkeley Unified School District adopted a new district-wide sexual harassment policy, which defined sexual harassment as "unwelcome sexual advances, requests for sexual favors, and other verbal, visual, or physical conduct of a sexual nature."

Think about those defining characteristics. And remember, as you think, that we live in a society which, for hundreds, perhaps thousands, of years, has been structured upon the idea that males initiate sex. Males, in our society, are expected to make sexual advances and issue requests for sexual favors. Traditionally—for untold thousands of years—in our society the rule has been: if you're a man, you go out and search for a woman who appeals to you; then you make your move—you "come on to her," you "make a pass at her," you make a sexual advance. Traditionally—for untold thousands of years—in our society the rule has been: if you're a woman, you wait for a man who appeals to you to make a sexual advance; if no man who appeals to you does make a sexual advance, you use your feminine wiles to try to influence a man who does appeal to you to make such an advance. These are your options.

Now, the Berkeley School Board has, in effect, made it illegal to make an unwelcome sexual advance or an unwelcome request for sexual favors. What is a man, in our society, to think in response to a policy like this? Can you really blame him if he thinks, Yeah, but how do you know a sexual advance or a request for sexual favors is unwelcome until you've made it? After all, in our society, women are encouraged never to make it unequivocally clear to any male that they enjoy or welcome his sexual attentions. For a woman to do so would be to admit that she is a "slut."

But, in these circumstances, how is your average—or even above- or below-average—male to know that his sexual advances or requests for sexual favors are unwelcome? He finds out by making them. If he is rejected, they are unwelcome. If they are not, he's home free. Except . . .

It's also a universally known and universally understood rule of our society that sometimes when a woman says no, what she really means is, "I'm a bit surprised or taken aback, and I need time to think about this, but . . . maybe. Ask me again. Show me that you really want me."

So . . . if you're a male in this society you learn that rejection only means you should try again *at least one more time*—after all, if you don't show her you're really interested in her, and aren't defeated by a little difficulty in your path, why do you expect her to respond to you?

Then, one day, you run afoul of the PC sexual harassment police. And you suddenly realize that a perennial issue in interpersonal, intersexual relations which has for centuries been relegated to the realm of manners or civility—the issue of how men and women sort out how who is attracted to whom and who will go to bed with whom—is now being settled in courts of law. What were formerly regarded as issues of etiquette—issues of concern to people in general and to oneself in particular to the extent that one hopes to maintain a reputation for good manners and civility in one's society—are now regarded as issues suitable for adjudication by the state.

The evidence of this has been everywhere over the past half dozen years. In Sonoma County, California two former emergency-room nurses filed suit, claiming the bawdy jokes told by their female nurse supervisor a few years before amounted to sexual harassment. In Los Angeles County a federal judge had to rule that the "quiet reading" of *Playboy* magazine did not create a sexually harassing atmosphere in county fire stations. Also in Los Angeles County, two separate sexual-harassment suits were filed against a councilman who had cursed at City Council meetings where women were present.

Nor is "sexual harassment" the only example of this trend. Nearly fifteen years ago, back in 1984, "Gentle Reader" posed the following question to Miss Manners in that columnist's then-current *Guide to Excruciatingly Correct Behavior*: "Are there legitimate rules about non-smokers telling smokers when and where to smoke?"

"Yes," replied Miss Manners.

> Smoking should be confined to certain parlors to which the smokers may retire from the sensible people and make their disgusting mess. One should not smoke at the same table where others are still eating. If you wish to smoke in the presence of clean people, you must ask their permission and be prepared to accept their refusal to grant it.

"Even the most vehement opponent of smoking could subscribe to such rules," commented J. Russell King in a *New York Times* article in November 1984.

> But many smokers do not consistently subscribe to them, and as a result a growing number of people want this sort of question taken out of the realm of etiquette and brought into the realm of law.
>
> As those who do not smoke grow bolder toward those who do, cities and states across the country are coming under increasing pressure to enact legislation that restricts smoking in public and in the work place.

Well, I think we all know what has taken place on *that* front since the mid-1980s. Countless new laws and regulations have been enacted all over the country in an attempt to protect non-smokers from being *offended* by the behavior of smokers. God forbid that anyone should ever be offended. God forbid that anyone should ever be insulted. God forbid—but let Senator Carol Moseley-Braun of Illinois (a Democrat, if it matters) finish this thought. "A fundamental right," she told a National Urban League dinner in Washington early in August 1993, "is freedom from insult."

May I paraphrase? People ought to be nice. If they aren't, they should be prosecuted or sued. They should be taken to court for not being nice.

There is one place in the United States, but only one, as far as I have been able to ascertain, where this philosophy is being consistently carried out. In the town of Raritan, New Jersey, late in 1994, the borough council adopted an ordinance which forbade "noisy, rude or indecent behavior . . . using profane, vulgar or indecent language . . . [and] making insulting remarks or comments to others," either in public or in private.

Why is this kind of thing happening? Why are interpersonal matters that used to be regarded as matters of etiquette now being treated as matters best dealt with by legislators or courts of law?

The simple answer is: it's because public manners—civility, as it used to be called—have gone out the window in recent years.

Back in 1993, late in the year, at around the same time that the U.S. Supreme Court was awarding damages to a woman who hadn't been damaged, but only offended, by her boss's behavior, a Canadian reporter named Graham Fraser took a look at the issue of incivility in the United States for the *Toronto Globe and Mail*. Among the instances of incivility which he found south of the border were bumper stickers that read, "Don't Like My Driving? Phone 1-800-EAT-SHIT"; T-shirts that warned readers to "Bac the Fuc Up"; and radio personalities like Howard Stern who "shriek vulgarities and win huge audiences." Fraser interviewed Richard Mouw, the president of Fuller Theological College in Pasadena, California, and found him lamenting "the loss of civility, which he defines as 'public politeness, showing courtesy in the public square.' "[80]

Nor were such observations unique to seminarians and to those looking at U.S. society from outside it. In that selfsame year of 1993, Peggy Noonan, the GOP speechwriter who wrote "a thousand points of light" and "a kinder, gentler nation" for George Bush, announced her intention to develop a new show for PBS—a show about manners. Since I never watch PBS—and never miss it—I don't know whether Ms. Noonan's proposed program ever saw the light of day.

But I do know that her concern with manners was—and is—

shared by many others. Late in 1996, three full years after the gloomy observations of Graham Fraser, the ecclesiastical lamentations of Richard Mouw, and the posturings of Peggy Noonan, what the Associated Press described as "a group of 48 prominent intellectuals, journalists, historians and sociologists" convened at the University of Pennsylvania to discuss the " 'explosion of incivility' in American society and around the globe." The group, known as the Penn Commission on Society, Culture and Community, agreed to meet biannually through 1999 "to discuss the rising tide of rudeness and how to stem it."[81]

About a month later, early in 1997, the *San Francisco Chronicle,* echoing thoughts being expressed in many American newspapers, not infrequently in response to the news of the Penn Commission's creation, proclaimed that

> [t]he incivility that characterized the 104th Congress has been denounced from all sides . . . [but] [o]f course, the view outside Washington is no better. From schools to courtrooms to broadcast airwaves to neighborhood sidewalks and streets, rudeness and coarseness have become ever more prevalent.

Only a few days earlier, Ellen Goodman, the nationally syndicated *Boston Globe* columnist, had sounded a very similar theme. Her column focused on a friend who had "taken a vow of civility . . . after assorted encounters of the third finger kind with hostile drivers" and various other of the myriad unpleasantries of modern urban life. "Starting now," Goodman wrote, "she will not only ratchet up the pleases, thank yous and would-you-minds, but also the friendly eye contact and the small daily conversations that are so trivially labeled as 'mere pleasantries.' They do not seem so mere to her anymore." Goodman too had noticed the mounting chorus of criticism over

> the coarseness of public discourse, the rudeness of private life. . . . The calls for civility now come from left, right and center. In one radio address, the president called for greater civility in debate. And

before a law school audience last fall, no other than Justice Clarence
Thomas criticized "individuals who've forgotten the common standards of decency that every individual should show to others." . . .
The motto of the 1960s was "Tell it like it is." The motto of the late
1990s may yet become "Mind your manners."[82]

For, as civility has declined, the touchiness of those who
most lament its passing has steadily increased. "You'd think,"
Miss Manners wrote in a column published not long before
Goodman's, that "we were all 18th century aristocrats, ready to
pounce on the merest flicker of a hint as an intolerable insult to
be avenged with the sword." Think of the women who are ready
to pounce on the merest flicker of a hint as an intolerable
instance of "sexual harassment" to be avenged with the long arm
of the law. Think of the nonsmokers who are ready to pounce on
the merest flicker of a hint (a man with an unlighted pipe in his
mouth, for example) as an intolerable instance of violating their
airspace with "secondhand smoke"—and who, again, look to
government for redress of their grievance. Think of the teenagers
who make the evening news so regularly these days through their
readiness to pounce on the merest flicker of a hint as an intolerable instance of "disrespect," to be avenged with the nearest Uzi.
We are living in a society in which three closely related trends
seem to be unfolding all at once. First, manners and civility are
breaking down. Second, some people are attempting to address
this breakdown by calling for government action against the
impolite. Third, still others are imposing vigilante justice—typically, the death penalty—on those who treat them rudely. What
is going on here? How did we come to this pass?

These questions may be more easily addressed if we take a
step back from the journalistic immediacy of the subject matter
and reflect for a few moments about what "manners" and
"civility" are—where they come from, how they develop in a
society, and what social function they serve, if any.

The short answer to this cluster of more basic questions is

that manners is a code of conduct, a set of rules for "proper" or "appropriate" conduct, which arises spontaneously within a social group. Civility is the habit of obeying or exemplifying this code of conduct. When we say, then, that civility is declining in U.S. society, what me mean is that the individuals we meet—on the street; in stores, parks, and concert halls; in public buildings, at school, in workplaces—no longer live up to the standards set by what we have all learned over time is what it means to be "polite" or "courteous." We mean that more and more of the individuals we encounter—and especially the *strangers* we encounter—fail to behave in the way we have all been taught to believe they *should* behave; that is, a larger and larger percentage of the strangers we meet do not display good manners.

And what *this* means is that life goes much less smoothly for us than it otherwise might. "What life and society require of each of us," writes the early twentieth-century French philosopher Henri Bergson, "is a constantly alert attention that discerns the outlines of the present situation, together with a certain elasticity of mind and body to enable us to adapt ourselves in consequence."[83] Sociability, Bergson wrote, is elasticity, adaptability, a highly developed skill for adjusting smoothly to the ever-changing flux which is the network of all our associations with other people.

Over time, people have evolved general rules to facilitate this desired flexibility—rules most people have found useful in smoothing out the inescapable bumps, sudden stops, quick readjustments in speed, and so on that characterize human social relations. The name for this code of rules people have developed is *manners.* Like grammar, it is an instance of spontaneous order, an instance of an order that arose from the separate decisions and actions of millions of individuals without ever having been planned by anyone or even any committee. Like grammar, it is constantly changing, constantly adjusting to changes around it. What was standard English a generation or two ago may or may

not be standard English a generation or two later. What was good
manners in Queen Victoria's day is not in every respect the same
as what is considered good manners today.

But there is a certain fundamental logic behind grammar, a
logic that stems from the basic purpose which unites social users
of a language—that is, the desire to communicate a meaning
clearly to someone else. Similarly, there is a certain fundamental
logic behind etiquette, a logic that stems from the basic purpose
of users of codes of manners—that is, the desire to convey to
all—even those who look or act very differently, even foreigners
and worshipers of unknown and possibly bogus gods—an attitude of evenhanded consideration and respect.

It seems obvious enough why people in general would regard
this as a good sort of attitude to convey to the world at large. If you
come forward into society treating everyone with equal consideration and respect, you would seem to stand a much better chance
of avoiding discord and violence, a much better chance of per-
suading others to do your will, and a much better chance of doing
business profitably with others. Business always prospers best
where peace and harmony prevail. Manners are the spontaneously
evolved rules of promoting peace and harmony in social life.

This is not a new idea, of course. Listen to the late Henry
Hazlitt writing more than thirty years ago in his *Foundations of
Morality* (1964):

> It is true that a part of any code of manners is merely conventional and
> arbitrary, like knowing which fork to use for the salad, but the heart
> of every code of manners lies much deeper. Manners developed, not
> to make life more complicated and awkward (though elaborately cer-
> emonial manners do), but to make it in the long-run smoother and
> simpler—a dance, and not a series of bumps and jolts.[84]

Some two hundred years earlier, in 1752, David Hume had
this to say about manners in his *Inquiry Concerning the Principles of Morals*:

As the mutual shocks in society, and the oppositions of interest and self-love, have constrained mankind to establish the laws of justice in order to preserve the advantages of mutual assistance and protection, in like manner the eternal contrarieties in company, of men's pride and self-conceit, have introduced the rule of good manners or politeness in order to facilitate the intercourse of minds and an undisturbed commerce and conversation. Among well-bred people a mutual deference is affected; contempt of others disguised; authority concealed; attention given to each in his turn; and an easy stream of conversation maintained, without vehemence, without interruption, without eagerness for victory, and without any airs of superiority. These attentions and regards are immediately agreeable to others, abstracted from any consideration of utility or beneficial tendencies: they conciliate affection, promote esteem, and extremely enhance the merit of the person who regulates his behavior by them.[85]

Fifteen years after Hume's *Inquiry* came Adam Ferguson's *Essay on the History of Civil Society* (1767). Ferguson taught what the Scots of the time described as "natural philosophy" at Edinburgh; he wrote in this book of what later came to be called "spontaneous order." And one of the first things we notice in reading through Ferguson's *Essay* in search of illumination on the topic of manners is a distinction he makes about halfway through between "barbarous" or "rude" nations, on the one hand, and "civilized" or "polished" nations, on the other. (Notice, if you will, that "rude" is not only the opposite of "civilized" and "polished," but also of "civil" and "polite.")

And what is it exactly that characterizes those nations which Ferguson classifies as *"barbarous* or *rude"*? That the people of such nations are "vehement in their attachment to one society, and implacable in their antipathy to another." In a word, they are intolerant, bigoted, prejudiced, distrustful of anyone who looks different or behaves differently; their behavior is the opposite, not only of the POLIte, but also of the POLItic and the cosmoPOLItan—the qualities you need to live successfully in a POLIs, a city.

When one studies the famous barbarians of past ages, Ferguson writes, one learns that they "were bold and fearless in their civil dissensions; ready to proceed to extremities, and to carry their debates to the decision of force."

> They had no forms of expression, to mark a ceremonious and guarded respect. Invective proceeded to railing, and the grossest terms were often employed by the most admired and accomplished orators. Quarreling had no rules but the immediate dictates of passion, which ended in words of reproach, in violence, and blows.[86]

By contrast, says Ferguson, "the principal characteristic, on which, among modern nations, we bestow the epithets of *civilized* or of *polished*" is none other than "... the employing of force, only for the obtaining of justice, and for the preservation of national rights."[87]

This banishing of force from social relationships except for purposes of obtaining justice and preserving national rights, Ferguson argues, is necessary in order to achieve the ultimate end of civil society; "the happiness of individuals," he writes, "is the great end of civil society: for in what sense can a public enjoy any good, if its members, considered apart, be unhappy?"[88]

It is worth noting here that what Adam Ferguson had in mind by the phrase *civil society* seems quite close to what Edward Crane, David Boaz, and other writers associated with the Cato Institute, the Washington-based libertarian think tank, seem to have in mind when they speak—as they have quite frequently over the past few years—about "civil society." Boaz, in his book, *Libertarianism: A Primer,* writes that "[c]ivil society may be broadly defined as all the natural and voluntary associations in society."

"The associations we form with others," he writes, a little earlier on the same page,

> make up what we call civil society. Those associations can take an amazing variety of forms—families, churches, schools, clubs, fraternal societies, condominium associations, neighborhood groups,

and the myriad forms of commercial society, such as partnerships, corporations, labor unions, and trade associations.[89]

And, one might add, the rules that spontaneously emerge from such associations—rules of the sort we call *grammar* and *manners*. These, too, are a part of civil society.

Ferguson said little or nothing about the mechanism by which manners and civility develop in societies. Neither do Crane, Boaz, and their colleagues at Cato. But some illuminating comments have been made on this subject. Listen, for example, to William Graham Sumner, in his book *Folkways: A Study of the Sociological Importance of Usages, Manners, Customs, Mores, and Morals*:

> If we put together all that we have learned from anthropology and ethnography about primitive men and primitive society, we perceive that the first task of life is to live. Men began with acts, not with thoughts. Every moment brings necessities which must be satisfied at once. Need was the first experience, and it was followed at once by a blundering effort to satisfy it. It is generally taken for granted that men inherited some guiding instincts from their beast ancestry, and it may be true, although it has never been proved. If there were such inheritances, they controlled and aided the first efforts to satisfy needs. Analogy makes it easy to assume that the ways of beasts had produced channels of habit and predisposition along which dexterities and other psychophysical activities would run easily. Experiments with newborn animals show that in the absence of any experience of the relation of means to ends, efforts to satisfy needs are clumsy and blundering. The method is that of trial and failure, which produces repeated pain, loss, and disappointments. Nevertheless, it is a method of rude experiment and selection. The earliest efforts of men were of this kind. Need was the impelling force. Pleasure and pain, on the one side and the other, were the rude constraints which defined the line on which efforts must proceed. The ability to distinguish between pleasure and pain is the only psychical power which is to be assumed. Thus ways of doing things were selected, which were expedient. They answered the purpose better than other ways, or with less toil and pain. Along the course on which efforts were compelled to go, habit, routine, and skill were developed. The

struggle to maintain existence was carried on, not individually, but in groups. Each profited by the other's experience; hence there was concurrence toward that which proved to be most expedient. All at last adopted the same way for the same purpose; hence the ways turned into customs and became mass phenomena. . . . In this way folkways arise. The young learn them by tradition, imitation, and authority.[90]

"It is of the first importance to notice," Sumner continues, a page later,

that, from the first acts, by which men try to satisfy needs, each act stands by itself, and looks no further than the immediate satisfaction. From recurrent needs arise habits for the individual and customs for the group, but these results are consequences which were never conscious, and never foreseen or intended. They are not noticed until they have long existed, and it is still longer before they are appreciated. Another long time must pass, and a higher stage of mental development must be reached, before they can be used as a basis from which to deduce rules for meeting, in the future, problems whose pressure can be foreseen. The folkways, therefore, are not creations of human purpose and wit.[91]

One thing remains to be said about the role of manners and civility in society, it seems to me, before we can profitably return to where we began—to the current breakdown in civility in our own society and the ways in which people are attempting to deal with it. That something is said best, perhaps, by Albert Jay Nock, who wrote about social and political questions in this country from just before the beginning of World War I to around the end of World War II. In an essay called "A Study in Manners," published in the 1920s, Nock had this to say:

The word *manners,* unfortunately, has come to be understood as a synonym for deportment; it includes deportment, of course, but it reaches much further. Properly speaking, it covers the entire range of conduct outside the regions where law and morals have control.[92]

Moreover, says Nock,

[i]t is interesting to remark that a sense of manners, delicacy of perception in matters of conduct, and the strength of character which regularly and resolutely enforces upon oneself their findings, seem to attain their best development in the absence or abeyance of law. Our Indian hunting tribes, for example never formed a State, and lived without law or government; and there is no end of testimony to the extraordinary and impressive development of manners and the sense of manners, that prevailed among them.[93]

Near the end of his essay, Nock comments further on this point:

Once we give up the pestilent assumption that the only effective sanctions of conduct are those of law and morals and begin to delimit clearly the field of manners, we shall be by way of discovering how powerful and how easily communicable the sense of manners is, and how efficiently it operates in the very regions where law and morals have so notoriously proven themselves inert. The authority of law and morals does relatively little to build up personal dignity, responsibility and self respect, while the authority of manners does much. The sacrifices and renunciations exacted by the one authority differ in quality from those exacted by the other, and one assents to them in a different spirit. In a habitual and sensitive regard to the demands of manners, one "lives from a greater depth of being." All this is a matter of experience; anyone can try it for himself and find out that it is so. The trouble is that an enormously exaggerated stress on law and morals gives little encouragement to make the trial. It is easier, in a society like ours, to do as the rest do, and mechanically refer all conduct to the sanction of law and morals without troubling oneself to question its applicability or to cast about for a more appropriate authority.[94]

What I think Nock is referring to here is the fact that most people obey the law or what they have been told are fundamental moral precepts because they have been ordered to do so—and even then, they do so only occasionally, because, even in the far-from-perfect United States of seventy-five years ago, the law did not yet prescribe and restrict individual behavior so lavishly that one ran into legal or moral rules at every turn. It was only occasionally that one confronted situations in which one was tempted to break either a law or a fundamental moral rule. But it was every day, many times every day, that one was challenged to mind one's manners. And one comes, after years of this, to obey manners out of deeply ingrained habit; one comes, after a while, to have difficulty even imagining behaving otherwise than one is expected to behave according to the code of manners one has long lived with. The habits of a lifetime—or even a fraction of a lifetime—of honoring and observing civility inculcated within a person will insure that that person almost automatically, unthinkingly, behaves with consideration and respect toward all comers. A lifetime—or even a fraction of a lifetime—of doing no more than the law requires an individual to do in his or her relations with other people will probably insure the death of civility within the society in which that individual lives.

Look around you at what is happening in our society, even as I speak. Since Nock wrote on the role of manners in society some seventy-five years ago, there has been a tremendous growth in the extent to which law affects the everyday life of the average person. On every level of government in our society—local, state, and federal—the sheer number of laws on the books has vastly increased, and so has the number of types of activities and situations which have been brought under the purview or jurisdiction of the law. Today, one runs afoul of the law constantly. Today, one runs into situation after situation, far more than merely once a day, when one is tempted for one reason or another to break the law.

When the number of laws on the books greatly increases, and when the "reach" of the law—the spheres of human activity which fall under the law's purview—greatly expands, it becomes more and more difficult to enforce all laws equally. Law-enforcement officers have to prioritize. They have to decide which laws are more important than others, and therefore which laws most deserve—and least deserve—enforcement. In this sort of environment, in which the frequency of the temptation to break the law is already increased, because the law has intruded itself into so many areas of human life, it must also become easier and easier to break the law with impunity. Since it is impossible to enforce all the laws equally without recruiting half the population as police officers, it becomes easier and easier to break laws—especially laws most people recognize as petty and trivial—and get away with it.

But if it is relatively easy to break the law with impunity in a society such as ours, how much easier it is to commit a lesser offense—a breach of manners, for example—and get away with it! Naturally enough, then, people begin to commit such breaches in steadily growing numbers with every passing day. And, because they have grown up in a society in which it tends to be taken for granted that the only remedy for offenses or transgressions of any kind is government action—laws or lawsuits—the response to this decline in civility by those who deplore it is to call for laws and to file lawsuits. And, of course, the further growth of government that occurs in response to these calls only promotes, rather than retarding, the already generally prevailing mood of tastelessness, vulgarity, rudeness, and lawlessness. Turning to government for redress of grievances against the rude is, then, not only ineffective, but actually counterproductive. It tends, in the long run, to produce more, rather than less, of the behavior it is intended to wipe out.

A point very similar to this one is made in a recent essay by James Dorn of the Cato Institute. The essay is called "The Rise of Government and the Decline of Morality." In it, Dorn treats manners as a subcategory of morality, exactly as Henry Hazlitt did in his 1964 book, *Foundations of Morality.* This is in contradistinction to the approach taken by Albert Jay Nock, in his essay "A Study in Manners." Nock distinguishes manners on the one hand from law and morals on the other hand.

But set these petty differences—as I truly believe they are—
aside. Both Hazlitt and Nock distinguish between the sphere of
manners and the sphere of law. So does James Dorn.

"The growth of government," Dorn writes, "has politicized
life and weakened the nation's moral fabric."

"The most obvious signs of moral decay in America," he
writes, a little farther on in the essay,

> are the prevalence of out-of-wedlock births, the breakup of families,
> the amorality of public education, and the eruption of criminal
> activity. But there are other signs as well: the decline in civility, the
> lack of integrity in both public and private life, and the growth of lit-
> igation as the chief way to settle disputes.[95]

Note the first item Dorn chose to list after the phrase "But
there are other signs [of moral decay] as well": "the decline in
civility." Later in his essay Dorn returns to this point when he
writes that "[t]he welfare state has attenuated private property
rights and weakened the informal rules of manners and morals
that make life worthwhile."

Dorn is, of course, operating here from within the same network of assumptions and ideas that inform his colleagues, Crane
and Boaz, when they talk about "civil society." Dorn never says
so in so many words, but he seems to grasp—intuitively, if not
explicitly—that manners is one of the devices by which spontaneously ordered civil society organizes and governs itself.

Through such devices as its codes of manners, civil society
promotes the view that you are responsible for yourself, that it is
up to you to get yourself a living however you can, and that you
would be well advised to treat others fairly and respectfully,
because, if you impoverish yourself by failing to do so, you will
have no one to fall back on (other than such friends and family
members as might choose to come to your aid). You're on your
own. So says civil society.

Government—the chief spokesman for political society—

promotes the view that you are *not* responsible for yourself; you are a "product" of society. Most likely, you are a "victim." But whether you are or aren't, society is responsible for you. You have a "right" to decent housing, adequate transportation and medical care, and nutritious food. In effect, the world owes you a living. You don't have to do anything in return. You don't even have to keep a *civil* tongue in your head.

So why should you? After all, the reason you wanted to be civil in the old days was the penalty—ostracism, which could have extremely adverse economic consequences. Today, you don't have to live up to anybody's standards of polite behavior to get a living. Today, the world owes you a living, remember? And today, if anyone should choose to fire you or cease doing business with you or otherwise refuse to associate with you because of your bad manners, government has seen to it that you can haul that former employer or business associate or landlord into court for "discriminating" against you and thereby violating your "civil right" to other people's time and property.

All this goes some distance toward accounting for our current civility problem. But, to return to our starting point, certainly another factor is decadence. In decadent periods such as the one we have all been living through since the mid-1960s, the normal influence of cultural norms, standards of behavior, and the like, is weakened, so that, while most citizens go right on living as they have always been expected to, a larger and larger minority dissent more or less openly, embracing unorthodox ideas, lifestyles, and standards of behavior.

By praising decadence, as I am doing in this book, and by praising the individuals who have the guts to fly in the face of orthodoxy and go their own ways, I do not mean to imply that orthodoxy is always wrong and that alternative ways are always right and always better. Many of the alternative medicines and sciences that were enthusiastically explored by the '60s generation were follies, and their new adherents might well have been

better off blindly following an orthodoxy they didn't comprehend. And, of course, the overall quality of life of an entire
society can be eroded significantly by an atmosphere which
encourages ignoring the duly constituted authorities in whatever
field. In a period of decadence, the duly constituted authorities
on manners are just as suspect as the duly constituted authorities
on everything else. What we see around us is, I fear, in part a by-
product of the decadent spirit which I still fundamentally admire
—a reminder, if you will, of the costs of freedom.

18

A Tale of Three Decades

And the future, then? What does it hold for American society? In 1968, Lyndon Johnson resided in the White House, Earl Warren presided over the U.S. Supreme Court, Dean Rusk ran the State Department. Students were demonstrating on the nation's campuses, police were rioting in the streets of Chicago. *We Are the People Our Parents Warned Us Against* by Nicholas Von Hoffman held a spot on the nonfiction bestseller lists, as did Norman Mailer's *Armies of the Night* and Tom Wolfe's *Electric Kool-Aid Acid Test.* A series of articles in the *Nation* by a San Francisco Bay Area historian named Theodore Roszak was creating quite a stir in the intellectual world. It would create an even bigger stir a year later when it reappeared, greatly expanded, as a book, under the title *The Making of a Counter Culture.*

What fiction were people reading? John Updike's *Couples,* Lawrence Durrell's *Tunc,* Donald Barthelme's *Unspeakable Practices, Unnatural Acts,* James Gould Cozzens's *Morning Noon and Night.* Thornton Wilder was the winner of that year's

National Book Award for fiction. On campus, where paperbacks were more in demand (and readers were much more numerous), it was mostly (though certainly not entirely) books of a few years and, in a few cases, a few decades before that were turning heads and shaping attitudes: Joseph Heller's *Catch-22,* Robert A. Heinlein's *Stranger in a Strange Land,* Kurt Vonnegut's *Cat's Cradle,* Ken Kesey's *One Flew Over the Cuckoo's Nest,* Anthony Burgess's *A Clockwork Orange,* J. R. R. Tolkien's *Lord of the Rings,* Hermann Hesse's *Steppenwolf* and *Siddhartha,* J. D. Salinger's *Catcher in the Rye,* George Orwell's *1984* and *Animal Farm,* and the works of Ayn Rand, Alan Watts, and Timothy Leary (whose most sensational book yet, *The Politics of Ecstasy,* had only just been published).

The same kids were listening to Bob Dylan, the Doors, and the Grateful Dead, as well as to the Beatles (whose "Lady Madonna" and "Hey Jude" were among the year's biggest hits) and Simon and Garfunkel. Moviegoers were flocking to see *Funny Girl* with Barbra Streisand, *The Lion in Winter* with Peter O'Toole and Katharine Hepburn, and *2001: A Space Odyssey.* All the rage on TV were *Bonanza* and a new CBS offering, an investigative news program called *60 Minutes.*

More than half a million Americans were in Vietnam fighting a war that increasingly seemed both interminable and unwinnable. More than five hundred of them were coming back in boxes every month. Ronald Reagan was governor of California. Jimmy Carter would soon be governor of Georgia. Garry Trudeau was still at Yale. The most popular and controversial of the political cartoonists who roamed the comics pages rather than the editorial pages back then was a man named Al Capp, whose strip related the doings of a genial hillbilly called Li'l Abner.

The question is, how much have things really changed since then? Nicholas Von Hoffman is still with us—on the nation's op-ed pages and in the nation's bookstores. Tom Wolfe is still selling books. So are Joseph Heller, Kurt Vonnegut, Robert A. Heinlein,

J. R. R. Tolkien, J. D. Salinger, George Orwell, and Ayn Rand. Ronald Reagan and Jimmy Carter, now former presidents as well as former governors, remain important national figures. Dylan, the Doors, and the Dead are still selling records, as are the Beatles and Simon and Garfunkel. Barbra Streisand still draws at the box office, as does science fiction. *60 Minutes* still draws on TV. *Star Trek,* which was a prime-time network TV series in 1968, is one of the champions of the box office in 1998.

Garry Trudeau has replaced Al Capp, of course; Mike Doonesbury has taken over from Li'l Abner. Lucas, Spielberg, and Co. have transformed the film industry. But even on the surface, on the level of what names figure importantly in politics and popular culture, more has stayed the same since 1968 than has undergone any important change. And if you look beneath the surface of things, if you look into the values and beliefs that determine the fundamental character of both politics and popular culture, you'll find that, for all practical purposes, we're still in 1968.

The sum of such values and beliefs is sometimes called the *Zeitgeist,* the spirit of the age. Taste in ideas, politicians, the arts, and entertainment constitutes a kind of public display of whatever that spirit is—whatever general attitude toward the human condition prevails. When large numbers of individuals express enthusiasm for a particular film or TV series or novel or musical work, you can expect to find certain of the fundamental values of that society reinforced, defended, and generally upheld by that work.

Or, to put it another way, the writers who gain the widest fame and favor with the public in any given period are the writers who do the best job of reflecting back to that public whatever are its own major preoccupations—the ideas, the dreams, the notions of what things in life are the most and least important, most and least worthy of a person's attention and concern. The same may be said of the journalists, advertising men, and filmmakers who attain the greatest popularity in any given period. We can learn something about the underlying philosophy of an era even from those products of the era that seem to contain no ideas or "meaning" in the usual sense—from trends in architecture and interior design, for example, and from trends in musical taste.

And, as I have pointed out, the trends in politics and popular culture that we see around us today are substantially the same as the ones we saw around us in 1968. Many of the same politicians, artists, and entertainers who were hogging attention thirty years ago are still hogging attention today. And newcomers to the political and cultural spotlight are sharing that spotlight because their work is of the same general type—expresses the same general belief system, the same general sense of values—as the work of the oldtimers. The meddlesome, war-mongering, lavishly spendthrift administration of Lyndon Johnson has thus given way to the equally meddlesome, somewhat less bellicose, but even more lavishly spendthrift administration of Bill Clinton.

To understand why this cultural and political continuity is so striking, reflect on the contrast between popular culture in 1938 and 1968. It's a dramatic contrast. The New Deal has given way to the Great Society. The gritty realism of Ernest Hemingway, James T. Farrell, and John O'Hara has given way to the satiric, romantic, and surrealistic fantasy of Vonnegut, Tolkien, and Barthelme. Benny Goodman and Glenn Miller have given way to Dylan, the Doors, and the Dead. The conformist, team-playing young adults of the Great Depression and the World War II years have become the mystified, alienated parents of the '60s, unable either to comprehend or to tolerate the styles and folkways of their adolescent offspring.

No such "generation gap," as it used to be called, exists for the parents and kids of 1998—at least, to nothing like the same extent. There is always a gap between generations, of course; that is an inescapable part of the human condition. Yet consider the results of the latest annual survey of the attitudes and views of the nation's college freshmen, released on January 12, 1998 by researchers at the American Council on Education and

UCLA. Nearly 350,000 freshmen took part in the survey, which was conducted in the fall of 1997 at 665 colleges and universities. "Its size and scope are unrivaled," wrote Rene Sanchez of the *Washington Post,* "and [for the past 30-odd years] its results have . . . been used to gauge how new college students view their lives and their futures."

Were the baby boomers—the parents of these new college freshmen—profoundly unimpressed with the offerings of the colleges and universities in which most of them were enrolled thirty years ago? Have they, in the years since, demonstrated a marked disinclination to participate in the political process at all—for example, by ignoring their "right to vote" in record numbers? According to Sanchez,[97] this latest survey of college freshmen portrays its respondents as "more bored with school . . . [and] less interested in politics . . . than any other class in a generation."

"The results of the survey are quite dismal about politics," Sanchez wrote, farther on in the article. Only "about 27 percent of [the freshmen] say that 'keeping up to date with political affairs' is important. At the start of the decade that percentage was above 40 percent." Moreover, "[o]nly about 17 percent of this year's college freshmen expressed interest in 'influencing the political structure.' "

Still, strikingly, the freshmen do exhibit a kind of political enthusiasm for one issue—an issue that was also popular thirty years ago with their parents. "An increasing number of freshmen," Sanchez wrote, ". . . want marijuana legalized—35 percent now, compared with 17 percent in 1989."

The young people of today also more commonly agree than disagree with their parents about music, fiction, TV, movies, and the like. The rock stars of the '60s, for example, enjoy a status with the young people of the '90s that the big bands of the '30s and '40s never enjoyed with the young people of the '60s. "Contrary to the wishes of buttoned-up types of all ages," James Sullivan wrote in the *San Francisco Chronicle* for June 22, 1997,

the hippie legacy is alive and well today, having permeated our popular culture in the 30 years since the [1967] Summer of Love.

Conventional wisdom says the cultural revolution was a bust:
Relaxed sexuality led to sexually transmitted diseases. Mind expan-
sion led to the Manson family. Rock 'n' roll experimentation led to
the interminable blues guitar solo.

Countless pop "movements" of the past 30 years have actively
antagonized the legacies of the Summer of Love: Glam mocked the
earthy clothes, punk mocked the spacey formlessness, goth mocked
the sunny dispositions.

And yet the hippie era's many badges remain integral parts of
the pop uniform. From multiple-attraction carnival-style tours to
homespun shows with patrons sitting cross-legged on the floor, the
tribal mentality of the Summer of Love persists.

And this is the considered judgment, not of a wistful baby
boomer longing nostalgically for the days of yore, but of a professional writer who specializes in popular music and popular
culture and who was only two years old when the Summer of
Love took place.

Another recent survey of the college freshmen of 1997–98
sheds further light on the current younger generation's cultural
preoccupations. This one was conducted among students in
freshman writing classes at the University of California at
Berkeley in the fall of 1997. The results were released in mid-
January 1998. Three of the ten "most popular authors" among
these young readers were J. D. Salinger, George Orwell, and Ayn
Rand. The same three authors placed in the top ten the last time
this survey was taken at Berkeley, back in 1987. The three "most
popular books" among freshmen in 1987 were *The Color Purple*
by Alice Walker, *The Fountainhead* by Ayn Rand, and *Catcher
in the Rye* by J. D. Salinger. The three most popular books in
1997 were *The Fountainhead* by Ayn Rand, *Catcher in the Rye*
by J. D. Salinger, and *The Hundred Secret Senses* by Amy Tan.

Why have we had such relative continuity and stability in our
popular culture over the past thirty years? Partly because the

same people who determined the character of popular culture in the '60s are still determining it today—the members of the 75-million-strong baby boom generation. During the '60s, when the leading-edge baby boomers were in high school and college, they created a new youth culture that has since become the basis for the dominant culture in our society. It was the baby boomers who made the '70s the "Me Decade" through their devotion to self-realization and self-fulfillment. It was the baby boomers who made the '80s the era of the Yuppie. Since the 1960s, this generation has made each successive decade of American life its own; expressive, through sheer weight of numbers, of the values and beliefs of *this* generation, rather than any other.

Similarly, the politics of 1998 is being made by the same people who were responsible for the politics of 1968—the parents and grandparents of the baby boomers. Politics in modern America is always dominated by the spirit of the older, property-owning generations, for these are the people who vote most actively. If a large enough proportion of the older generation participates in elections, it can assert its values over those of the younger generation, even when the younger generation is much larger in sheer numbers.

So it has been that, since the 1960s, the generational values of the baby boomers' parents have continued to prevail in American politics. Though more numerous than any previous generation, the boomers themselves have tended to participate even less in politics than previous generations did. Though the leading-edge boomers, now in their forties and fifties, have certainly entered the ranks of the older and the property-owning, they have lagged behind previous generations in their level of involvement in the political process. Moreover, those members of the baby boom generation who have already enjoyed successful political careers have been those members whose sympathies were most in line with those of the older generation. Bill and Hillary Clinton are excellent cases in point. They are baby boomers, but their political values are those of the generation that preceded them, the generation that was running things when Bill and Hillary were young. This is why there is so little substantive difference between the administration of Bill Clinton and the administration of Lyndon Johnson.

Of course, on another level entirely, the Clintons are quintessential baby boomers: Hillary the political activist, dedicated since her college days to the ideals of the New Left, eternally oblivious to the fact that those ideals have never won genuine acceptance among the American public, not even in their apparent heyday thirty years ago; Bill the do-your-own-thing hedonist, dedicated since his college days to the anthem of the sixties—sex, drugs (though he didn't inhale, of course), and rock 'n' roll—gladhanding his way into one powerful position after another in order to enjoy the gratifications such positions make it so easy to obtain—faithfully, if half-heartedly, following the policy prescriptions of his wife and longtime political partner in the process.

When asked to rate their satisfaction with the performance of a sitting president, Americans are influenced at least as much by their sense of political theater as by their positions on specific policy issues or their notions of what the Republican and Democratic parties "stand for." They have continued to favor Bill Clinton with higher performance ratings than Ronald Reagan or George Bush ever won, and they have continued to do so despite his various peccadilloes, because they *like* Clinton better, in precisely the same sense and for precisely the same reasons that they like one film or one novel or one TV show better than another—because the one they like better feels more comfortable, more like family, more in tune with their own feelings and ideas about the way the world is, the way life is, and what is important about both. To a population dominated numerically by members of the baby boom generation, Bill Clinton has to seem a more comfortable figure than either Ronald Reagan or George Bush, not only because of his more or less open hedonism, but also because he seems so much less rigid and uptight and authoritarian than either of his predecessors. (It is presumably this selfsame image, by the way, which so inflames and animates Clinton's many rabid opponents, since his policies differ only incrementally, if at all, from those of Reagan and Bush).

The values and beliefs of the baby boom generation are likely to come into full domination of American political life only after the turn of the century, perhaps even as late as 2010—if they are ever to achieve such dominance at all. If they do, we are likely to see a rather different sort of president in the White House—different, that is, from Lyndon Johnson, Bill Clinton, or any of the current leaders of the Republican and Democratic parties.

Why? Because the essential element in the culture of the baby boom generation is a tolerant, even welcoming attitude toward diversity and eclecticism, a tendency to favor individuality of style and to applaud the willingness to differ from the majority, the usual, the norm. This is the generation, after all, whose fundamental attitude toward the human condition has been summarized—and accurately—as an injunction to "do your own thing." This is a generation that considers it both natural and desirable for a gathering of people to be a gathering of many diverse styles, a generation uncomfortable with uniformity and the idea that it is in some way wrong to deviate from whatever happens to be the dominant style of one's time.

Consider the results of a September 1997 poll of the political opinions of "Digital Citizens" or "the Connected"—the predominantly baby-boom-generation-and-younger denizens of the Internet—commissioned by *Wired* magazine. "Digital Citizens are markedly libertarian," the magazine reported. While their

> political values draw heavily from the humanism and social tolerance of the left . . . they dispute the view that government is both primarily responsible for and effective at confronting and solving social problems—a cornerstone of both the Democratic Party and the ideology we've come to call liberalism.[98]

Moreover, though 40 percent of the Connected describe themselves as Republicans (while only 33 percent call themselves Democrats), more than 70 percent adopt a strikingly un-Republican position on medical marijuana: they favor legalizing it. Also somewhat un-Republicanly,

> more than half believe it's possible to cut military spending by a third and still maintain current levels of national security.
>
> Meanwhile, twenty percent of the Connected prefer to call themselves independent. This is a group that thinks for itself and decides issues one by one, instead of following a strict ideology or platform. . . .
>
> What Digital Citizens reject, the survey suggests, isn't civics or two-party politics, but rigidly formalized authority. This new culture represents a political community with a strong sense of adventure and exploration . . . they have little admiration for those [politicians] who blindly adhere to party platforms or stiffly parrot what their political handlers tell them.[99]

This attitude is, at root, an individualistic attitude. It is even, in a broad sense, as *Wired* acknowledges, an implicitly libertarian attitude—for the only way each individual *can* enjoy the freedom to do his own thing is if society as a whole is freed from coercion.

It is no accident that Ayn Rand was one of the most popular authors of the past three decades, or that, as has been noted, the past three decades have seen the rise of a number of prominent libertarian journalists, including at least two syndicated columnists and a number of important opinion editors and writers. It is no accident that the modern libertarian intellectual and political movement has experienced steady and rapid growth in both size and public visibility and influence in the years since its birth in 1968 and 1969.

It is no accident either that the authors and musicians who have won and held public favor over the past thirty years have been the most individual, the most experimental, and the most eclectic in their fields. Rock music itself, the characteristic music of our era, is a hybrid form, the product of an eclectic borrowing and mixing of elements from two types of music that were kept strictly, even fiercely, segregated within living memory—white country music and urban black music.

The films of the past three decades have certainly persuaded the conservatives that Hollywood is firmly committed to the ideology of "do your own thing"—and not without reason, either. Network TV, by contrast, is no more committed to individualism today than it ever was. But what has been the result of that failure by network TV to keep up with the times and the changing cultural values of its audience? Network TV has seen serious erosion of its audience, as the members of the baby boom generation have made cable TV, VCRs, and satellite technology into booming industries by seeking ways to circumvent those networks and get both a greater variety of video programming and increased individual control over what is viewed—and when. The do-your-own-thing generation has demanded, and the market has supplied, a means whereby every individual can more easily so his own thing when it comes to video entertainment and information.

When *Time* magazine's Pulitzer Prize–winning culture critic, the late William A. Henry III, published his last book-length jeremiad about the state of our culture, *In Defense of Elitism,* back in 1994, he noted this individualistic tendency. He decried the "self-absorbed and inward-looking" way in which contemporary Americans now pursue entertainment;[100] he deplored the popularity of music videos, which, he wrote, appeal to "the personal dreamscape of individual viewers who find their own meaning or at least feeling in each vignette";[101] he railed against those members of the mass media who, instead of treating the activities of mainstream, establishment scientists as the only activities worthy of coverage, "give a respectful place at the table to creationists, faith healers, herbalists and homeopaths, new age crystal worshippers, and other practitioners of magic and mumbo-jumbo."[102] (Could it be that the media people in question have grasped that Americans of today want to make up their own minds about such matters rather than being told what to think?) Then, incredibly, only a few pages after issuing these complaints, Henry intoned that "[t]he missing element in every phase of American life . . . is what used to be called rugged individualism. This sort of frontier self-reliance is utterly out of fashion."[103]

Wrong, Mr. Henry. Come out of your study and look around you. Individualism *is* in fashion—never more so. As a society, we are still riding a wave of individualism that we first caught thirty years ago. Don't be discouraged by the so-called rise of the New Right—it makes so much noise in an effort to convince you that it's bigger than it really is—and by the likes of Bill Clinton and Janet Reno—they're the last, doddering specimens of what has been; they aren't the future, they're the past. Those of us who celebrate individuality, freedom, and diversity may take heart. The trends are in our direction, not in theirs. The future is ours.

Notes

1. Landon Y. Jones, *Great Expectations: America and the Baby Boom Generation* (New York: Coward McCann & Geoghegan, 1980), p. 2.

2. The term "minarchist" was coined in the late 1960s by Samuel Edward Konkin III, libertarian agitator, pamphleteer, and educator *extraordinaire.* Konkin, who is currently president of the Agorist Institute and editor of the *Agorist Quarterly,* used the word (as have several major mainstream publications, including *Newsweek,* since then) to describe those libertarians who advocate a severely limited government (though scarcely any government at all by today's standards) rather than the total absence of government advocated by their fellow libertarians.

3. William O. Reichert, *Partisans of Freedom: A Study in American Anarchism* (Bowling Green, Ohio: Bowling Green University Popular Press, 1976), p. 6.

4. Stephen L. Newman, *Liberalism at Wit's End: The Libertarian Revolt against the Modern State* (Ithaca, N.Y.: Cornell University Press, 1984), p. 50.

5. Reichert, *Partisans of Freedom,* p. 2.

6. Ibid.

7. Henry David Thoreau, *Civil Disobedience.*

8. Lysander Spooner, "No Treason No. 6," *The Lysander Spooner Reader* (San Francisco: Fox & Wilkes, 1992), p. 78.

199

9. Ambrose Bierce, *The Devil's Dictionary* (New York: Dover Publications, 1958), p. 101.

10. Milton Viorst, *Fire in the Streets: America in the '60s* (New York: Simon & Schuster, 1979), p. 166.

11. Newman, *Liberalism at Wit's End,* p. 27.

12. Murray N. Rothbard, "Liberty and the New Left'" *Left and Right* (Autumn 1965): 36, 39.

13. Carl Oglesby, "The World Before Watergate," *Inquiry* (May 29, 1978): 14.

14. Reichert, *Partisans of Freedom,* p. 553.

15. Ayn Rand, *For the New Intellectual: The Philosophy of Ayn Rand* (New York: Random House, 1961), p. vii.

16. Ayn Rand, *The Virtue of Selfishness* (New York: New American Library, 1964), pp. 144, 146, 148.

17. Ibid., p. 126.

18. Ibid., pp. 124–25.

19. Ibid., p. 146.

20. Ibid., p. 147.

21. Ibid., p. 148.

22. Ibid., p. 149.

23. Ibid., p. 151.

24. Ibid., p. 152.

25. Paraf-Javal, from his book *The Absurdity of Politics,* quoted in *Quotations from the Anarchists,* ed. Paul Berman (New York: Praeger, 1972), p. 60.

26. Jones, *Great Expectations,* p. 287.

27. Marilyn Ferguson, *The Aquarian Conspiracy: Personal and Social Transformation in the 1980s* (Los Angeles: J. P. Tarcher, 1980), p. 194.

28. Robert LeFevre, "Autarchy," *Rampart Journal of Individualist Thought* (Summer 1966): 6.

29. Ferguson, *The Aquarian Conspiracy,* p. 192.

30. Ibid., p. 240.

31. Kirkpatrick Sale, *Human Scale* (New York: Coward, McCann & Geoghegan, 1980), pp. 427–28.

32. David Boaz, ed., *Left, Right & Baby-Boom: America's New Politics* (Washington, D.C.: Cato Institute, 1986), p. 3.

33. H. L. Mencken, "The Fringes of Lovely Letters," in *Prejudices: Fifth Series* (New York: Octagon Books, 1977), p. 197.

34. Quoted in Max Nordau, *Degeneration* (New York: Appleton, 1895), p. 301.

35. Christopher Lasch, *The Culture of Narcissism: American Life in an Age of Diminishing Expectations* (New York: Norton, 1979).

36. Nordau, *Degeneration*.

37. Letty Cottin Pogrebin, *Family Politics: Love and Power on an Intimate Frontier* (New York: McGraw-Hill, 1984), p. 2.

38. Sar A. Levitan and Richard S. Belous, *What's Happening to the American Family?* (Baltimore: Johns Hopkins, 1981), p. 4.

39. Jonathan Gathorne-Hardy, *Marriage, Love, Sex and Divorce* (New York: Summit Books, 1981), pp. 292–93.

40. Richard Sennett, *The Fall of Public Man* (New York: Knopf, 1977), pp. 180–81.

41. Levitan and Belous, *What's Happening to the American Family?* p. 30.

42. Ibid., p. 180.

43. Andrew J. Cherlin, *Marriage, Divorce, Remarriage* (Cambridge, Mass.: Harvard University Press, 1981), n.p.

44. Levitan and Belous, *What's Happening to the American Family?* p. 30.

45. Cherlin, *Marriage, Divorce, Remarriage*, pp. 72–73.

46. Ibid., p. 75.

47. Ibid., n.p.

48. Levitan and Belous, *What's Happening to the American Family?* p. 172.

49. Karen Lindsey, *Friends as Family* (Boston: Beacon Press, 1981), pp. 1–2.

50. Jeane Westin, *The Coming Parent Revolution* (Chicago: Rand McNally, 1981), n.p.

51. Levitan and Belous, *What's Happening to the American Family?* p. 180.

52. Pogrebin, *Family Politics*, n.p.

53. John B. Rae, *The Road and the Car in American Life* (Cambridge, Mass.: MIT Press, 1971) p. 361.

54. David Laird, "Versions of Eden: The Automobile and the American Novel," *Michigan Quarterly Review* (Fall 1980/Winter 1981): 640.

55. Robert L. Heilbroner, "Halfway to the Moon on Wheels," *Petroleum Today* (Spring 1960): 2–3.

56. A. Q. Mowbray, *Road to Ruin* (New York: Lippincott, 1969), p. 240.

57. Ibid., p. 86.

58. Michael L. Berger, *The Devil Wagon in God's Country: The Automobile and Social Change in Rural America, 1893–1929* (Hamden, Conn.: Archon Books, 1979), p. 207.

59. Mark H. Rose, *Interstate: Express Highway Politics, 1941–1956* (Lawrence, Kans.: Regents Press, 1979), p. 3.

60. Mowbray, *Road to Ruin,* p. 203.

61. Rae, *The Road and the Car in American Life,* p. 224.

62. Ibid.

63. Jones, *Great Expectations,* pp. 38–39.

64. Rae, *The Road and the Car in American Life,* p. 252.

65. William Severini Kowinski, "Suburbia: End of the Golden Age," *New York Times Magazine,* March 16, 1980, p. 17.

66. Rae, *The Road and the Car in American Life,* p. 249.

67. Ibid., pp. 249–50.

68. Ibid., n.p.

69. Ibid., p. 256.

70. Ibid., p. 221.

71. Ibid., p. 357.

72. Ibid., p. 364.

73. Quoted in Leah Garchik, "Personals: Sex Guru Defends Bob Packwood," *San Francisco Chronicle,* September 27, 1995, p. E8.

74. Debra J. Saunders, "Touchy-Feely About Being Too Touchy-Feely," *San Francisco Chronicle,* December 11, 1992, p. A28.

75. "Harassment: His and Hers," *Harper's,* March 1993, n.p.

76. Ibid., p. 24.

77. Reynolds Holding, "New Weapons to Fight Sex Harassment," *San Francisco Chronicle,* January 24, 1994, n.p.

78. Quoted in Dianne Hales and Robert Hales, "Can Men and Women Work Together? Yes, If . . . ," *Parade,* March 20, 1994.

79. Ibid.

80. Graham Fraser, "Sticks, Stones, and Now: Growing Vulgarity," *San Francisco Examiner* (reprinted from the *Toronto Globe and Mail*) November 4, 1993, p. C4.

81. Associated Press, "Meeting Monday to Mull the Meaning of Meanness," *San Francisco Examiner,* December 8, 1996, p. A4.

82. Ellen Goodman, "An Outcry for Civility," *San Francisco Chronicle,* January 2, 1997, p. A19.

83. Henri Bergson, *Laughter: An Essay on the Meaning of the Comic,* trans. Cloudesley Brereton and Fred Rothwell (London: Macmillan, 1913), p. 18.

84. Henry Hazlitt, *The Foundations of Morality* (Irvington, N.Y.: Foundation for Economic Education, 1964), p. 75.

85. David Hume, *An Inquiry Concerning the Principles of Morals* (New York: Liberal Arts Press, 1957), pp. 83–84.

86. Adam Ferguson, *An Essay on the History of Civil Society* (New Brunswick, N.J.: Transaction, 1980), p. 198.

87. Ibid., p. 200.

88. Ibid., p. 58.

89. David Boaz, *Libertarianism: A Primer* (New York: The Free Press, 1997), p. 127.

90. William Graham Sumner, *Folkways: A Study of the Sociological Importance of Usages, Manners, Customs, Mores, and Morals* (New York: New American Library, 1960), pp. 17–18.

91. Ibid., p. 19.

92. Albert Jay Nock, "A Study in Manners," in *On Doing the Right Thing and Other Essays* (New York: Harper & Brothers, 1928), p. 187.

93. Ibid., pp. 192–93.

94. Ibid., pp. 200–201.

95. James A. Dorn, "The Rise of Government and the Decline of Morality," *Cato's Letter #12* (Washington, D.C.: Cato Institute, 1996), p. 1.

96. Ibid., p. 8.

97. Rene Sanchez, "College Freshmen Called the Laziest in a Generation," *San Francisco Chronicle*, January 12, 1998, p. A4.

98. Jon Katz, "Netizen," Online. Internet. Available: http://www.hotwired.com/special/citizen/.

99. Ibid.

100. William A. Henry III, *In Defense of Elitism* (New York: Doubleday, 1994), pp. 181–82.

101. Ibid., p. 183.

102. Ibid., p. 189.

103. Ibid., p. 209.

Index